AF477954

THE ART OF THE CITY

The Art of the City

RAFFAELE MILANI

Translated by Corrado Federici

McGill-Queen's University Press
Montreal & Kingston · London · Chicago

ISBN 978-0-7735-5133-6 (cloth)
ISBN 978-0-7735-5235-7 (ePDF)
ISBN 978-0-7735-5236-4 (ePUB)

Legal deposit fourth quarter 2017
Bibliothèque nationale du Québec

First published by Società editrice il Mulino, 2015, as *L'arte della città*.

Printed in Canada on acid-free paper that is 100% ancient forest free (100% post-consumer recycled), processed chlorine free.

The translation of this work has been funded by SEPS Segretariato Europeo per le Pubblicazioni Scientifiche, Via Val d'Aposa 7 – 40123 Bologna, Italy seps@seps.it – www.seps.it

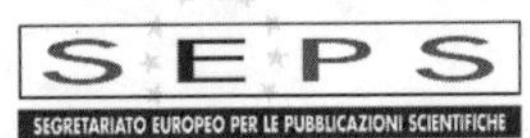

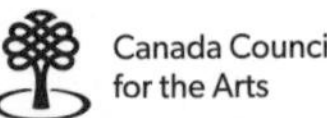

We acknowledge the support of the Canada Council for the Arts, which last year invested $153 million to bring the arts to Canadians throughout the country.

Nous remercions le Conseil des arts du Canada de son soutien. L'an dernier, le Conseil a investi 153 millions de dollars pour mettre de l'art dans la vie des Canadiennes et des Canadiens de tout le pays.

Library and Archives Canada Cataloguing in Publication

Milani, Raffaele
    [Arte della città. English]
        The art of the city / Raffaele Milani ; translated by Corrado Federici.

Translation of: Arte della città.
Includes bibliographical references and index.
Issued in print and electronic formats.
ISBN 978-0-7735-5133-6 (cloth). – ISBN 978-0-7735-5235-7 (ePDF). –
ISBN 978-0-7735-5236-4 (ePUB)

    1. City planning. 2. Cities and towns. 3. Architecture and society. 4. Art and society. I. Title. II. Title: Arte della città. English

NA9050 M5513 2017   711'.4   C2017-905391-4
                                           C2017-905392-2

This book was typeset by True to Type in 11/14 Sabon.

Contents

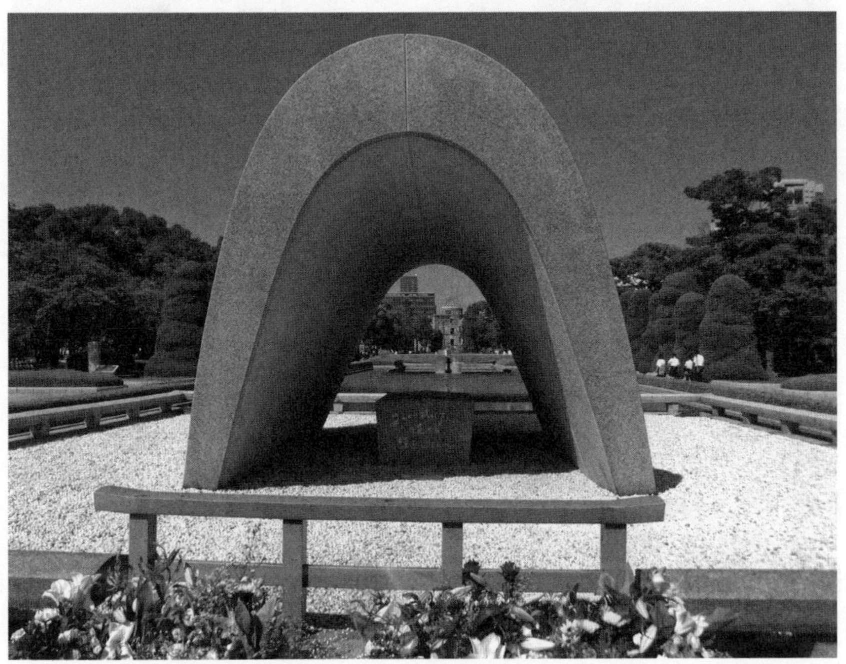

1 Hiroshima, Peace Memorial

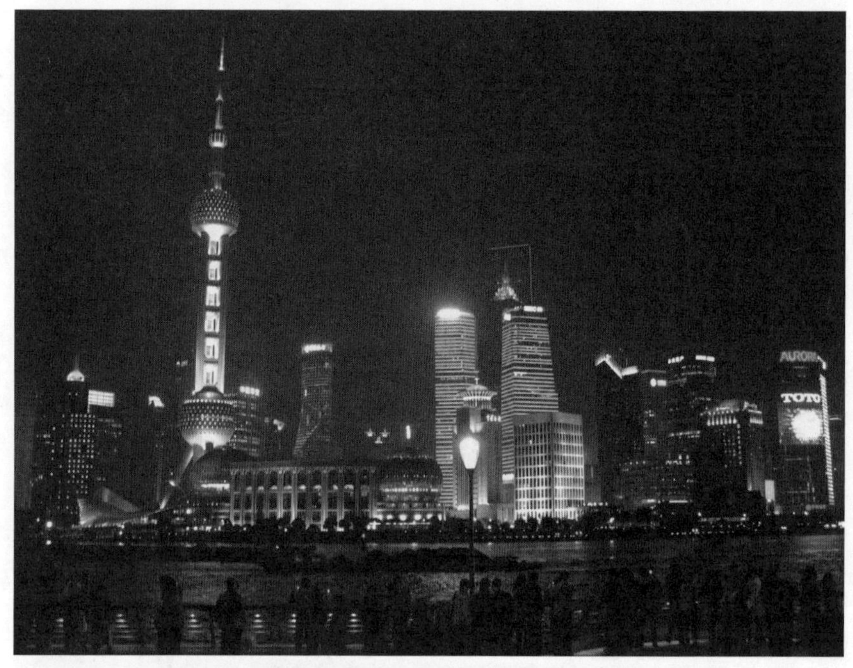

2 Shanghai, Pudong New Area

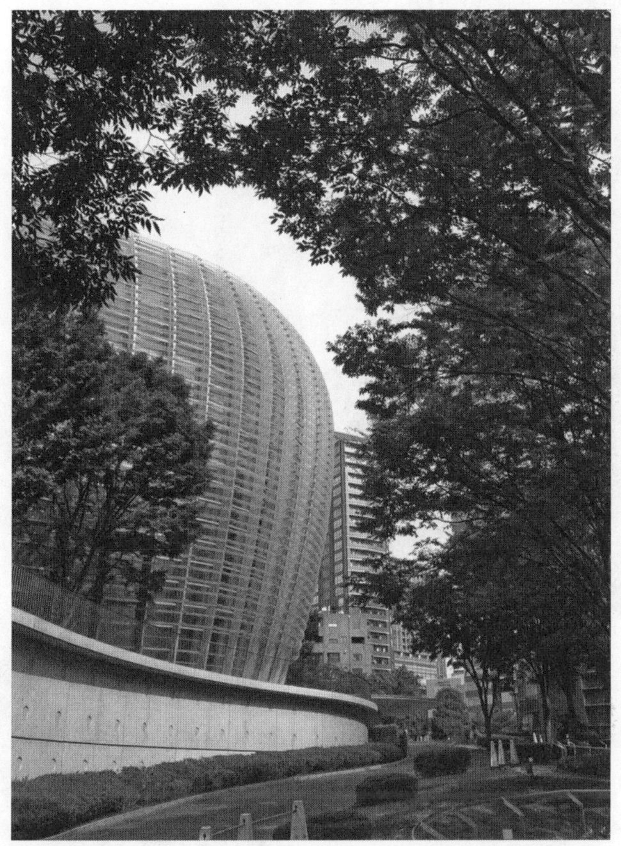

3a Tokyo, National Arts Center in Roppongi (architect Kisho Kurokawa, 2007)

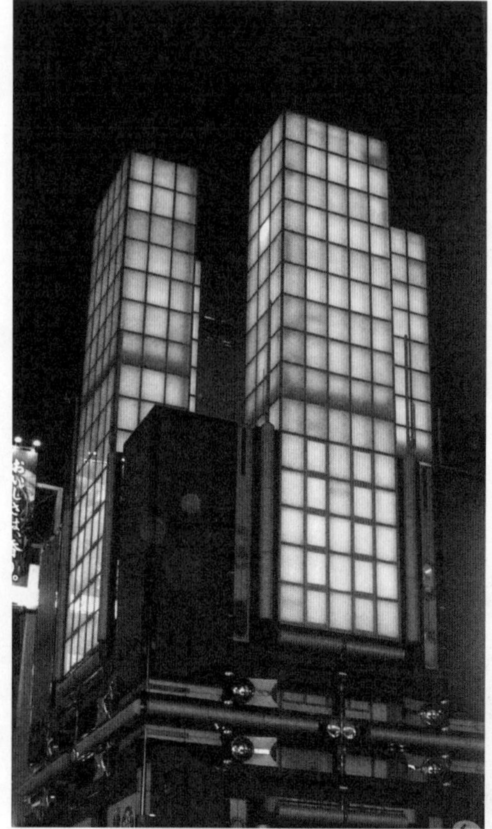

3b Tokyo, new architecture

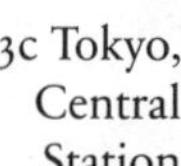

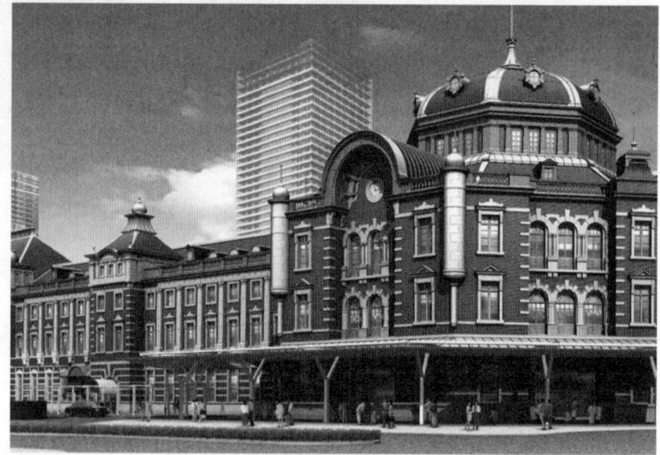

3c Tokyo, Central Station

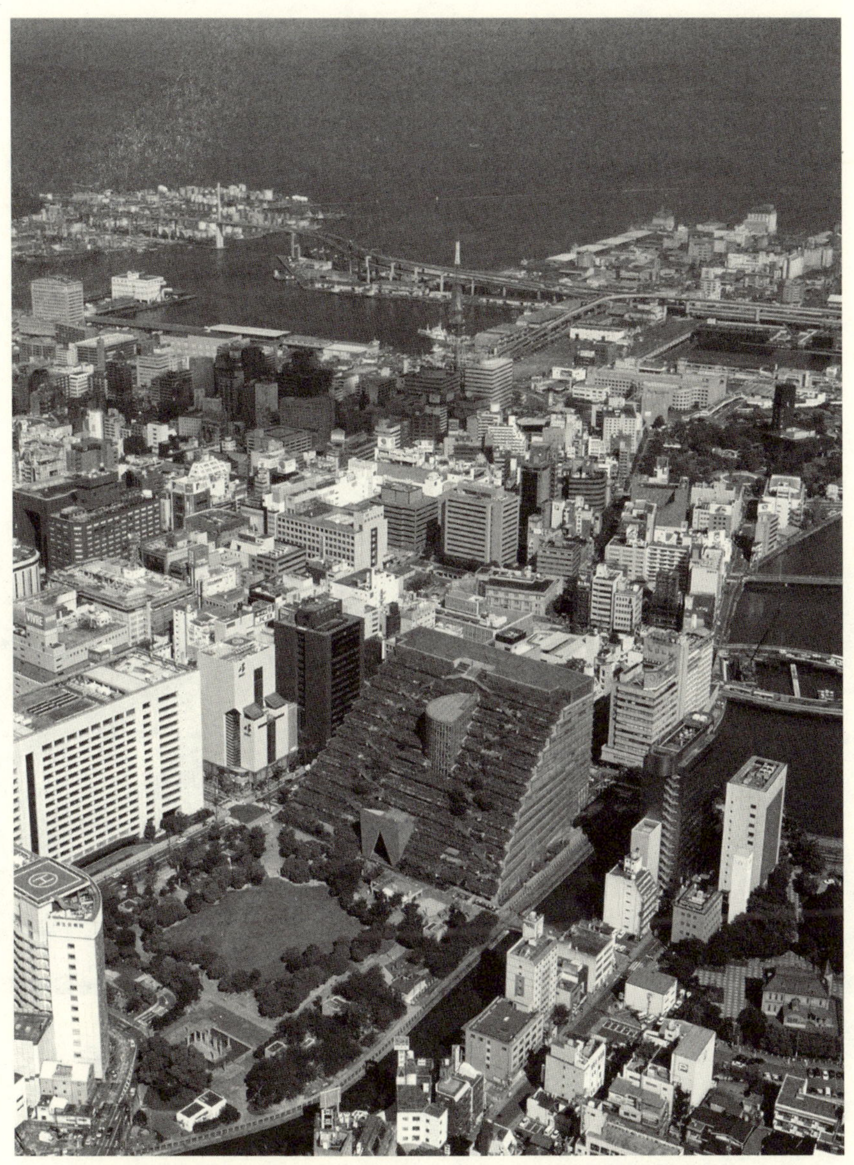

4 ACROS building in Fukuoka (architect Emilio Ambasz, 1995)

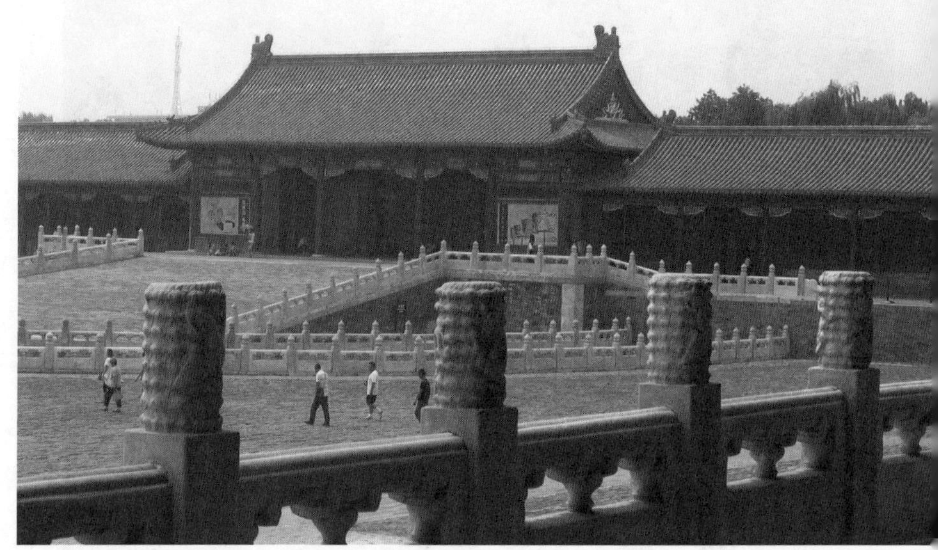

5a, 5b Beijing, Forbidden City

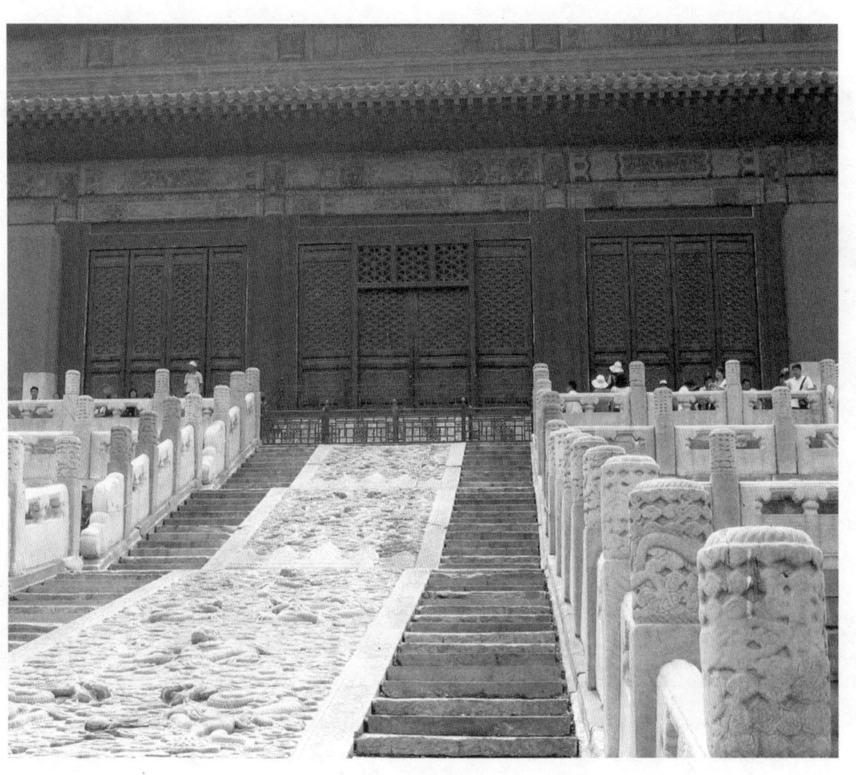

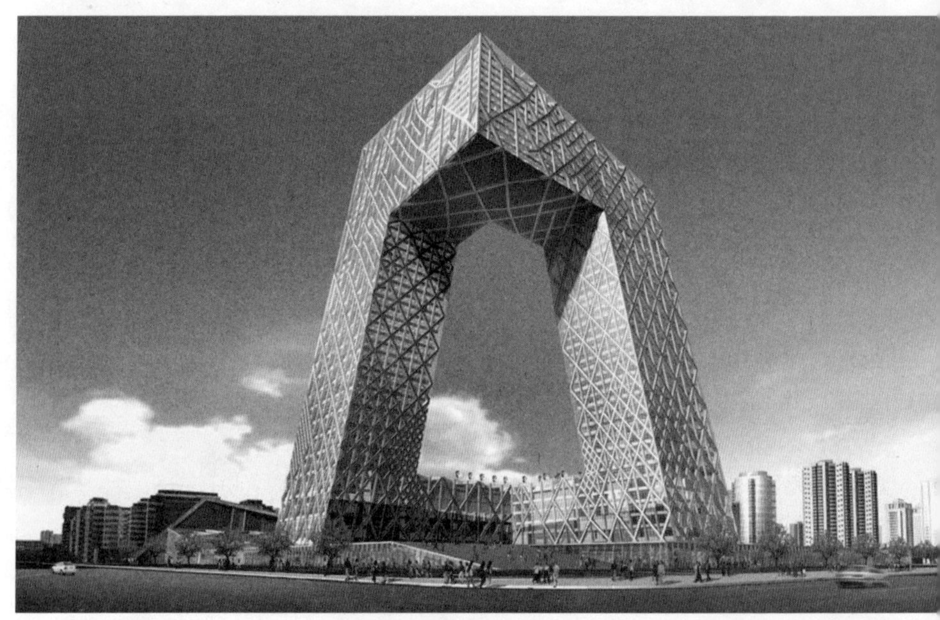

6a, 6b New Beijing, skyscraper, CCTV Headquarters (architects Rem Koolhaas and Ole Scheeren, 2006)

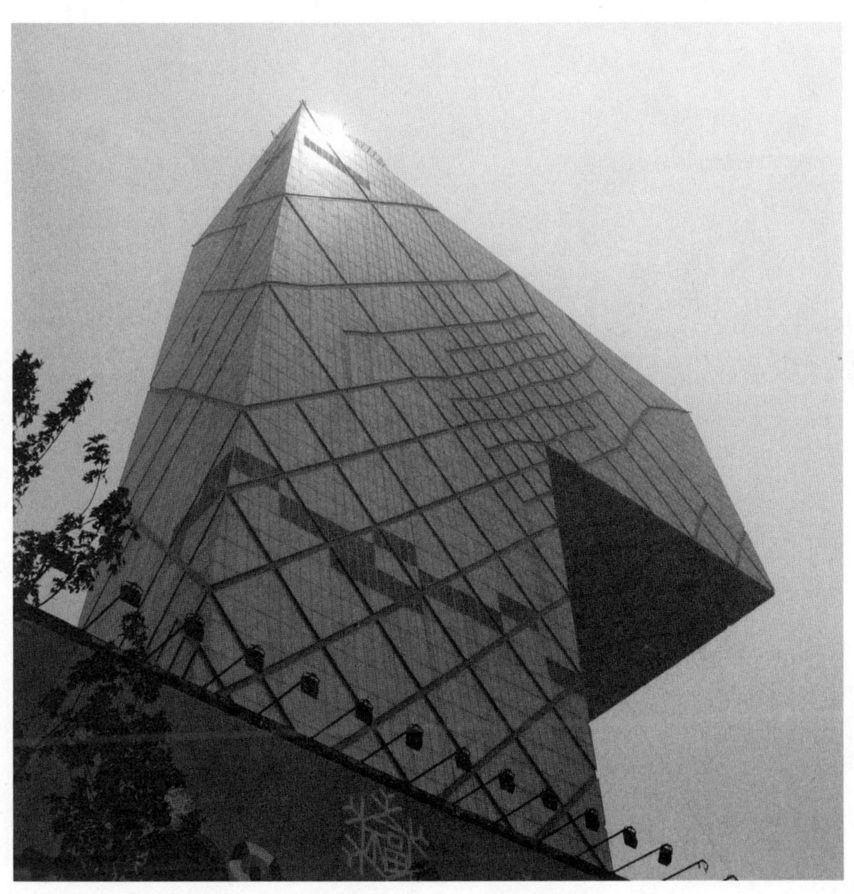

THE ART OF THE CITY

Introduction

The city is in me, like a poem
For which I have not yet found the words.
J.L. Borges, "Vanilocuencia" (Verbosity)

A product of history, culture, and civilization, the city appears to us initially as a celebration of the process of building, involving a play of forms and solids, or as a celebration of architecture. It is also subsequently perceived as a sign of communities and relationships, of which the forms are the expression. If we reflect on its meaning from ancient to modern times, the city represents a composite of human activity, an extraordinary map of collective and individual actions, the effect produced by an art of extended space. That composite interacts with the art of the landscape because it offers evidence of dedication, traces of fantasy, imagination, design, and objects created out of necessity. Analogous to the creation of cultivated fields, we can argue that there exists an art of the city that is the product of communities and individuals, architects and artists, city planners, labourers, citizens, and their political representatives – in other words, the product of an ideal and civil effort. It is also a concrete, multifaceted manifestation of the utilization of space, influenced throughout history by various social groups or ideologies. As Oswald Spengler writes in *The Decline of the West* (1926), all the great civilizations were urban civilizations. The central feature of "world history," which includes that of nations, states, politics, religions, the arts, and the sciences, is the story of humankind as the builder of cities. As Spengler writes:

> But the real miracle is the birth of the *soul* of a town. A mass-soul of a wholly new kind – whose last foundations will remain hidden from us forever – suddenly buds off from the general spirituality of its Culture. As soon as it is awake, it forms for itself a visible body. Out of the rustic group of farms and cottages, each of which has its own history, arises a *totality*. And the whole lives, breathes, grows, and acquires a face and an inner form and history. (1981, vol. 1, 90–1)

Proceeding from here and going beyond the house, temple, cathedral, and palace, the city as a whole becomes the object of a language of forms, and of a history of style that can be found throughout the course of a given civilization.

In this book, aesthetics lies at the core of an analysis, description, and evaluation of a mosaic of situations – as it does for Ernst Cassirer and Georg Simmel. The book presents a network of representations, drawing on philosophy to describe its cultural complexity. Through the prism of a variety of readings, using both material and non-material terms, the art of the city refers to the work of a community and of individuals, as well as the fascination that this work engenders and the fear it inspires. What emerges is a vast and monumental portrait of conceptual, creative, and constructive power. In tracing the evolution of civilizations relative to one another and the development of architectural styles, from ancient to modern, the book seeks to provide a living portrait of humankind. Fantastic metropolitan vistas and intriguing forms of strange beauty appear before us, evoking scenes from films or literary passages. In the city, whose forms create suggestive and stimulating images of the world, we feel like protagonists on the world stage, and a new *flânerie* (aimless strolling) takes shape alongside the spectacle offered up by media, within an exciting, expressive, and communicative strategy.

In recent times, the progress of humankind appears increasingly damaged by the rapid, improvised, and unsettling growth of the city. In its wake, the external, "natural" environment almost disappears, devoured by concrete that extends in every direction, not only in massive tracts but also as an intricate web of arteries crisscrossing the city. In addition, half the population lives in enormous habitats, like pawns in an increasingly powerful, labyrinthine, and pervasive pattern of life and movement. In spite of this, we remain struck by certain extraordinary and original architectural works, as objects that were once unimaginable and which now inspire awe. The city is the theatre of representation, the media spectacle of power where architects and politicians compete for the trophy of success.

In the face of the prevalence of urban architecture, the sister arts, such as literature, painting, and music, seem to be in decline. These art forms, which have for so long been reassuringly stable, are being displaced by the erratic and frenzied rhythm of the growing urban space, characterized for the most part by a great confusion of forms. In the age of globalization, antiquity – with its variety of features that become superimposed over time, often with positive results – must compete with the impetuousness of modern times, which shun and humiliate it. Flourishes of postmodernism, deconstruction, and hybridism now dominate. Furthermore, the supremacy of urban art and architecture is increasingly notable over even photography and cinema. Some cities, however, in the wake of a contemporary myth of sensibility and taste, come across as cinematic, due to the atmosphere they exude. This is the case for New York, Singapore, Shanghai, Tokyo, Dubai, Kuala Lampur, Hong Kong, Chengdu, Chicago, and London. Other cities seem more suited to the literary and pictorial imagination: Paris, Rome, Buenos Aires, Madrid, Berlin, Prague, Venice, Amsterdam, Lisbon, Barcelona, and Istanbul. Architecture and the city itself prompt a pleasure that is ambiguous. An enigmatic beauty greets our eyes and evokes certain films or passages in literature in an exciting communicative process that is both material and immaterial.

The feverish development of the megacity, like the global metropolis, speaks to the struggle of the powerful to find an image to impose – in absolute terms – on the world as their personal symbol. It is a struggle for economic supremacy. Politicians, powerful managers, and architects adore the shock of the monumental, while on the contrary, citizens attempt to participate in their world creatively in order to humanize this tireless territorial *poiesis* (making or creating) through projects that find new uses for the city's empty spaces, for the benefit of society.

The city is the result of an ideal and common effort; it is alive in its various manifestations, both physical and non-physical: stones and institutions are its supporting columns. I use the expression "art of the city" to refer to a poetics of inhabited space, including the ethical, aesthetic, and affective aspects of an anthropological understanding of lived places. The term "poetics" is used primarily in connection with the act of people inhabiting the earth; there is a new *poiesis* today, that is, a new activity aimed at affirming the cathartic potential of architecture and urban planning in the face of the unsustainable depletion of the environment. In this sense, our inhabiting of the earth can become a permanent state of creation and sharing. Only in this way – that is, by going beyond Heidegger's position (which is otherwise quite valuable) – can humankind still inhabit the earth "poetically," as Hölderlin hoped.

The city, home to half the world's population, is not merely the realm of economics and citizenship, although these are very important and relevant factors, as suggested by Max Weber. It also consists of the frenzied perception of this lived space – a system of objects and a non-material web of communication in which we are prisoners, but of which we are also creative users. It is without question a myth, then, and seems to be a disappointment with respect to what we hope for when we think of the ideal of the *polis*. Yet it is also rich in hope if read in its vastness, from the monumental nature of the ancient to the power of the postmodern, its totality of objects, facts, impressions, and moods, ranging from the enthusiasm and fervour of city planners to the misery and pain of those who live there.

There is a negative aspect of building on the land, represented by the presence of extensive suburbs (*favelas*, or slums): built-up areas that are shapeless, chaotic, and contaminated. The city imagined by engineers, architects, and philosophers between the two world wars, as provided for in the Athens Charter of 1931, part of a plan to restore community spaces, appears to be utterly eclipsed. Today the perceptions and actions of the city's inhabitants, apart from so-called urban planning, are starting to play an important social role in defining the spaces in which people work, exercise their imagination, and live, so that these areas might become zones in which hope can grow for better planning in the future. When we discuss the contemporary megacity and see the brutal exploitation of the planet, to which we are tied by a natural sense of "property" or ownership, we cannot fail to recall the words of Hannah Arendt and her principle of political action. As she states, we are expropriated by the powerful and subject to the order imposed by the large industries or the will of political groups. After more than half a century from the time of those declarations (in the Athens Charter), we are still directly and indirectly ensnared in the web that is the organization and distribution of energy, services, and property, which blinds us to the fact that our city, our neighbourhood, and the environment around us have changed so much in a short period of time. At a certain point, the light of conscience begins to burn, signalling a dire situation: forces are destroying the places where we live, along with our memories. We may find and sense that everything has occurred almost imperceptibly, within the silence of institutions. The matter is all the more serious since it seems that the disasters that we witness, both large and small, are never a public responsibility.

This is a discovery made not only by philosophers, but also by individuals who try to imagine the ideal by moulding the real and amalgamating necessity and utopia. Through building, people seek out community; however, they do so in order to avoid being deprived of their sense of belonging to nature. In order to make the city truly a refuge and a place to admire, we need to understand the forms and meaning of social ties. Only in this way will we find the courage to explore various heterotopias, beyond the dominant *kitsch*, as well as modernist planning and post-industrial deconstruction. Similarly, it is possible to imagine the role that architecture can play. The city space is infinite and dominated by relationships, proximity, and juxtapositions. Perhaps we are dealing with an exhausted space today, the product of the impression of disorder, attrition, and abandonment that it generates.

For some time, a questioning gaze has been cast on the forms of the city, and this book seeks to provide some of the answers. In our age, what is the nature of the beauty of the inhabited earth? Does it still make sense to speak of beauty? For the city in the age of globalization, the site of multiple languages, peoples, and communications, what is the future projected by such concepts as the "slow town" and the "smart city"? What value does, or can, the ancient city still have? Does an art of the city exist? What does it mean? With this phrase, I am identifying a set of features and norms endowed with an intimate *aréte* (moral virtue). At times, the city seems to have an intelligent and sensitive spirit, and we sense the aura of the process of inhabiting. At other times, it appears to be a living organism. Whatever its nature, which is certainly double in that it is both intelligent spirit and material body, we are invited to imagine for it a politics of civilization.

In the Anthropocene epoch in which we live, virtual technologies are creating previously unimaginable relationships between people and material objects. Urban spaces, or the new cities, the sites of sea change, produce fast-moving and widespread material images. In a few years, these will be interchangeable with their *in vivo*, mobile holographic reproductions, which will be perceived directly. City squares, streets, buildings, surfaces, and objects, some common and others bizarre, will disguise their composition, be it matter or light.

In some instances, we will no longer be able to distinguish between reality and appearance. We will be placed in the interactive sphere between the object and its copy, thinking that we are the protagonists of a thrilling journey. Very soon we will see significant cognitive distortions caused by the invasion of icons fired into cyberspace by multinational corporations, prompted by the effect that human actions have on the ecosystem. New frontiers of virtual participation will tempt us to eliminate the space between citizens and institutions, formulating a new politics of power: authoritarian politics. In addition, given that the taste for and sense of beauty are rooted in the mind, museums of museums will soon be built, based precisely on the fact that holograms allow us to reproduce a manufactured object in empty space, making it seem as though it were in front of us. We will experience the luminous objects painted by a Leonardo or a Mantegna, and new optical illusions will emerge. As with works of art, rock stars, movie stars, and political icons will enter our homes, our rooms: they will be ubiquitous figures. The past will come back to life in the near future, which is to say, today, as in Adolfo Bioy Casares's prophetic 1964 novel *The Invention of Morel*, and in Emilio Greco's 1974 film version of the same. We will, therefore, live among phantasms of light as we attempt to safeguard our most intimate feelings.

But what is the value of viewing a work of art that has been "democratically" reproduced in a mobile hologram? This is the point. So, too, is the question we have been asking for some time: Has technology made us freer or more enslaved? It may be that the mobile hologram satisfies our desire to be omnipotent, to be like the gods. Real or fake solids and simulated harmonies will be the entertainment game used to shape knowledge, with the aim of creating a new aesthetics. The image of the real city will coalesce with that of the virtual city, and we will be immersed in it. The real and the virtual are key elements in this book, which explores urban civilization and architectural form in the third millennium.

Within this framework of deep and tumultuous transformations, I would like to conclude by praising the work of Emilio Ambasz, whose projects point to a bright future for sustainable architecture and cities.

I would like to thank the following people for their most valuable suggestions: Pier Luigi Cervellati, Laura Falqui, Franco La Cecla, Lorenza Pignatti, Joseph Rykwert, and Stefano Scagliola.

I

The City as Habitat

BEFORE THE CITY: FOUNDATION MYTHS

Archival research enables us to produce a hypothetical reconstruction of the remote past. How can we think of the first human settlements without imagining our origins? We are compelled to imagine, in some way, the evolution of our species up to the one that preceded us and lived at the same time as our most distant ancestors. Lost in the mists of time, we are gripped by an intense interest in what might have been the earliest habitat, and we find ourselves moved at the sight of a hearth in a Neanderthal settlement, such as the one that Rem Koolhaas presented at the Venice Architecture Biennale in 2014, titled *Fundamentals*. Prior to the birth of the city, in the prehistoric times of hominid villages, we find the hearth, which not only represents the sense of place, but is also the symbol of the community of our ancestors, who took refuge in caves whose walls they decorated with paintings or carvings. The Biennale exhibition presented the discovery, made several years ago in Spain, of an ancient hearth, along with food scraps and ashes dating back approximately 228,000 years. Neanderthals decorated their objects of daily use but did not make paintings or carvings, which we find in abundance at the settlement sites of *Homo sapiens*. As Juan Luis Arsuaga states, representation is a feature of symbolic thought, creative language, and imagination, which are reflected in corresponding behaviours.

Indeed, it is as a result of this kind of thinking that we can examine the dawn of urban civilization and "feel at home" in it. But to which period does this apply? First of all, we need to keep in mind the distinction between *city* and *settlement*. I propose a conservative history. Some claim that the first city ever built was Klimonas in Cyprus, dating from 9000 BCE. Fifty years ago there was the discovery of Çatalhöyük in modern day Turkey by James Mellaart, dating to around 6000 BCE. In light of the recent discoveries by Vassil Nikolov, the first European city appears to be the vast fortified site in Provadia, Bulgaria, on the coast of the Black Sea, dating to around 4700 BCE. Prior to this, the first European city was considered to be Hamresanden in Norway, whose founding is said to have occurred in around 4000 BCE. Around the same time, however, the cities of Uruk, near the Euphrates River, and Jericho were established, which illustrates my remarks on the origins of the city. We should be aware that the features of the city are connected to the spread of agriculture, the stratification of society, and the specialization of work (market, exchange, primitive exploitation of natural resources, social roles, government institutions of the community, the functions of those conducting religious rituals), along with the organization of the spaces for the living and the spaces for burials and commemoration. As a whole, these factors imply non-absolute values that should be analyzed in the context of the civilization being studied. But we can trace with certainty the dawn of a sense of social belonging to the complex, built-up area of ancient settlements, and to the development of symbolic thought and language. In other words, we can trace the origins of the city to the way our brain processes information. In this regard, some researchers place the origin of language somewhere between the carving of geometric shapes on an ochre plate about 75,000 years ago in a cave in Blombos, on the South African coast, and the cave drawings made in the Franco-Cantabrian region around 40,000 years ago. From the cave drawings in particular we can infer the states of mind and the relationships involved with the first expressions of language. In the settlements of that period, an initial sense of community, facilitated by the instruments of communication based on symbolism, could have connected various functions that would later form the basis of what we now refer to as the city, the birth of which has been firmly established at around the year 4000 BCE.

When we talk about the birth of the city, we think of the Bible (specifically chapter four of the Book of Genesis), which recalls how Cain, an exile after killing Abel, founds a city to the east of Eden and gives it the name of his son, Enoch. At this place, for generation after generation, with the growth of humankind's penchant for violence following the original homicide, the weight of God's wrathful vengeance manifests itself in an endless cycle of conflicts and bloodshed. Cain represents the agricultural life, whereas Abel stands for the pastoral life. Abel is preferred to Cain perhaps because the latter offers to God the worst of the products of the earth. The murder sets off a tragic destiny. Some experts say that the Jewish city is the result of human labour, while the Greek city is, instead, a gift from the heavens to humankind. This view is reputedly supported by the myth of Amphion, who tames the boulders rising from the earth in order to build the walls of Thebes. It is for this reason that, among the Egyptians, it was rumoured that Amphion was a magician equal to Orpheus. The ritualistic killing, which is analogous to that of Osiris at the hands of Seth, or of Remus at the hands of Romulus, initiates what we refer to as the history of civilization.

In *City of God* (15, 5), Augustine of Hippo writes that the founder of the earthly city committed the first fratricide: he killed his brother, a citizen of the eternal city and a wanderer on the earth. In this text, it is not surprising that the capital of the earthly cities, Rome, the conqueror of so many peoples, is seen as an archetype. Even in this place, as Lucan notes, "the rising walls were wetted in a brother's blood" (2015, 95). We find other memorable pages in Livy's *Ab Urbe Condita* (History of Rome). Remus was killed by Romulus. As citizens of the earthly city, both brothers were acknowledged as the founders of the Roman state. In order to possess all the power, one eliminated the other. Along with the crime, its fame grew in wickedness; without the crime, the fame would have been diminished, though it would have been more "honest," according to Augustine. The case of Cain and Abel is different because the brothers did not aspire to possess the goods of the earth; here we see the birth of envy toward good people who extend the gift of charity to others. Sharing one's goodness with others is contrasted with possessing goodness but being unwilling to share it with others. Augustine goes on to clarify his point. What happened between Romulus and Remus shows how the earthly city has divisions within it, whereas what happened between Cain and Abel shows the contrast between the city of God and the city of humankind. In this Christian vision, we have opposition among evildoers on the one hand, and between the good and the evil on the other. In reality, there is no opposition among the good, if they are perfect. Cain and Abel, and Romulus and Remus, are two essentially symbolic duos that exemplify the web of violence that exists within the earthly city, and that characterize the history of the city of God, a land of exile, as well. I say exile because Cain's action has made it so. In Augustine's vision, the noble ideals of peace and goodness are distorted by the earthly city, torn apart by hatred and strife, and these distorted ideals bring death and false victories, which are acquired along the path to world domination. According to this view, urban civilization begins with a sacrificial victim and portends a future filled with tragic figures.

Various founding myths mix elements from different cultural and religious traditions. Reference has already been made to the Greek myths, that of Amphion in particular. In 1983, this myth was reinterpreted by Rosario Assunto, who compared it with that of Prometheus, pointing out in particular the dehumanization resulting from modernity. We have on one hand the city as a work of art and poetry, with a perfect balance of composition and meaning, an historical and cultural good, and on the other hand a "metropolis-macropolis-ecumenopolis" ruled by the principles of rationality and functionality, and associated with the machine of productivity, which is the result of science and technology. In contrast to the myth of the machine, we have the myth of harmony, symbolized by Amphion. Prometheus, who stole the secret of fire from the gods and revealed it to humans, is seen as being responsible for the damnation of humankind, resulting from the technological progress pursued across the centuries. Assunto's *La città di Anfione e la città di Prometeo* (*The City of Amphion and the City of Prometheus*) describes the natural disaster created by the industrialization we see all around us and attempts to inspire hope through nostalgia, suggesting that the future can revive aspects of antiquity. In fact, in the space of representation, the author situates the historic city, one that is rich in art and beauty, and in the space of utilitarianism, the industrial and post-industrial modern city. Across time, the urban form, which mirrors those who constructed it, undergoes change. It becomes an apparatus for the satisfaction of material needs; with the loss of the meaning of architecture, the idea of the city fades, as do its well-being and philosophy of life.

I am discussing myths concerning the dawn of urban civilization, but I could also mention the studies of Andrea Carandini or Joseph Rykwert (2002) on pre-urban Rome and the proto-history of the Campidoglio area of Rome, as suggested by the ruins associated with the legend of Saturnia. But I prefer to leave aside these considerations in order to deal with the fundamental theme of the city that revolves around the *nomos* (law or order) of Athens, a symbol of vastness, a spatial-temporal entity destined to set off a long series of meanings and events. Remaining within the topic of the myths of Greece and Athens, having already mentioned Prometheus and Amphion, I now turn to the story of Cecrops, half-man and half-serpent, the first king of Attica and the founder of urban society and its institutions, such as marriage, burial of the dead, and courts. He is also credited with the invention of writing and census taking. This is a very ancient reference. Related to this is the legend that Cecrops discovered male and female sexuality. In addition, he appears to be not only born of the earth but also associated with the profundity of Mother Earth. He is bimorphic, trimorphic, and androgynous. As an animal figure, he is associated with the serpent (ophiomorphism), a chthonic creature par excellence, belonging as he does to both the natural world and the under-world. For this reason, he represents the lack of distinction between the living and the dead. This complex figure is able to draw forth positive elements from mysterious nature for the benefit of the community, such as stability and fertility. The serpent is not to be driven away, as the sphinx is by Oedipus; instead, it lives on the Acropolis, venerated and nourished by the community (Herodotus, *Historiae*, VIII, 40, 2–3). Cecrops has the upper part of the male body and the lower part of the female body, thereby standing for both a distinction and a lack of distinction between the sexes, in the sense that awareness of the difference leads to marriage and the family structure: the original community cell. This myth does not die in the Athens of the fifth and sixth centuries, with the sophists and the reforms of Cleisthenes, Ephialtes, and Pericles. It survives secret-ly in famous discourses, often homilies, in memory of the fall-en. The Athenians felt united in their autochthony and the sense that they were born to honour their homeland. Thus, the *polis* is affected by the machine of myth-making, but the myth in the two instances described here is progressively dissolved by the privilege of citizenship, which was reserved for Athenians and not extended to foreigners. As Aristotle asserts: "Noble birth, in the case of a nation or State, means that its members or inhabitants are sprung from the soil" (1984, 1360b).

For the city to come into existence, however, the gods need to intervene. By dividing space, an entire universe arises. The first division of space produced the *temonos*, or sacred land cut off and assigned to the gods. This is described in reference to the *nomos* and its semantic indicators, as well as to the idea that Athens was considered a gift from the gods. The initial moment in the emergence of the *nomos* is associated with Cecrops and subsequently Athena, with Cecrops serving as witness. The fact that a god chooses to live there is a grace bestowed on that place and its inhabitants. In Athens there is a contest between Poseidon and Athena resulting from the assignment of the cities, which were to be dedicated to them. With a blow of his trident, Poseidon causes a sea to appear, while Athena takes possession of the city by planting an olive tree and calling on Cecrops to bear witness. A court of deities decides to award the city to Athena because Cecrops testifies in her favour. Filled with rage, Poseidon floods Attica. The *nomos* of Athens thus acquires cosmogonic value whereby the land (Athena) and the sea (Poseidon) are separated. Thus, the olive tree, symbolizing the land, is contrasted with the well containing sea water, both of which can be found on the Acropolis, because once his wrath subsided, Poseidon himself was able to become the protector of the community, and his cult was established on the Erechtheion. As we read in Pausanias, the olive and the well were still being displayed in the second century CE to commemorate the ancient contest. Because the olive tree was protected by both Zeus and Athena, Athens would be the scourge of enemy armies, as stated in Sophocles's *Oedipus at Colonus* (vv. 694–706). It is a tree that vanquishes the enemy cohorts. Sophocles also speaks of Athens as a gift from a great god and associates the olive tree with the oar, in order to indicate both rootedness in the earth and movement on the sea. The latter has no geographic boundaries and no specific features. The oar, in essence, must turn back into the tree. As Tiresias prophesied to Odysseus, after he was saved from the sea: "Then you must plant your well-shaped oar in the ground" (*Odyssey*, Book XI, v. 129). Despite the fact that its fate lies between the sea and land, Athens is definitely terrestrial. Themistocles and Pericles had chosen a naval strategy; in contrast, in 356 BCE, Isocrates equated marine *arche* (origin) with bad customs. In 350 BCE, Plato wrote his *Laws* (III, 705–7), in which, as he did previously in the *Timaeus* and the *Critias*, he compares the two destinies (favouring the terrestrial one) for the salvation of Athens. Now, however, the power of the original myth is waning. Not long after, the defeat at Chaeronea in 338 BCE would signal the political transformation of Greece.

I would add one more observation on the founding myth of Athens. Cecrops had three daughters: Aglaurus, Herse, and Pandrosus. As Stefano Scagliola (2013, 48) explains, the names are related to features of Mother Earth: Herse and Pandrosus to the dew that enables the earth to be fertile, and Aglaurus to that which shines, often in reference to water. This telluric aspect, however, which predates the polytheistic age, is eclipsed by a new mythologem in the case of Erechtheus, which initiates a male, rather than female, line. Divinity is integrated with the earth. Indeed, Erechtheus is born from the lock of wool containing the semen of the god Hephaestus, which Athena lets fall to the ground, having used it to clean her thigh after Hephaestus tries to rape her. Erechtheus is raised by Athena, who places the newborn in a basket, which she entrusts to Pandrosus, the child either assuming the form of a serpent or is enveloped by a serpent when the inquisitive sisters peer into it. Erechtheus is then raised within Athena's sacred enclosure and becomes the king who succeeds Cecrops. This is why the serpent has special importance for the city. Heroes and gods settle, creating a complex urban topography in which everything revolves around the Acropolis and the Erechtheion. Inside this temple we find the ancient wooden simulacrum of Athena, the sacred olive tree, the salt water well, the altar of Erechtheus, and the chthonic-Dionysian serpent. These are symbols of the forces creating the order of the world, and of the community that respects those same forces. Later, with Aegeus and Theseus, the *agora*, rather than the Acropolis, will become increasingly important, and a new public and cultural dimension will open up.

To this point, using a paleoanthropological, archaeological, and philosophical lens, I have schematically examined the period preceding the birth of the city and the earliest urban areas, in terms of their historical records, symbols, and mythologies. This is a world that stands in stark contrast to our modern one, which is represented by the megacity. Jacques Véron has stated that by 2030 more than 60 per cent of the people on the earth will live in cities. Barring an unimaginable catastrophic event, out of a total estimated population of eight billion, five billion will live in cities, two billion of which will live in the shanty-towns and slums of the megacities, especially in Africa and Asia. In times of social crisis, there is almost certainly the need for cooperation among people and the environment, and development that takes into account sustainable urbanization, as well as quality of life in the city. In light of such an emergency, we can look to the interesting studies of Stefano Boeri on the anti-city, or those of Franco La Cecla on urban planning – both critical analyses of urban development. Frustration and the integration of the new wretched of the earth are part of political action – or, to put it another way, political indifference. Furthermore, we see in the recent development of society the fraud of urban planning and the emergence of a new anthropology of dwelling, that is, technical knowledge juxtaposed with the culture of the city. A different perspective, one dealing with design theory and based on the "tradition of the modern" is offered by Vittorio Gregotti, who attempts to revive the fundamental principles of architecture in the age of the post-metropolis.

Regarding the instinctive need to live in communities, we could also ask ourselves what were and are the relationships between bodies and walls, which comprise the city. From the time of the earliest settlements, the effort or difficulty of nego-tiating the labyrinthine network of gateways, roads, and path-ways has been an issue, one reflected in the organization and the spatial segmentation of the urban layout. The need to orga-nize this urban layout was already evident between the third and the first millennium BCE, both in Hattusa, a horizontal city in Asia Minor, and Barumini, a vertical city consisting of *nuraghe*, or conical buildings with multiple towers, in Sardinia. Even today, if we think of the stratifications of the city's forms and the semiotics of the representations that these stratifica-tions inspire, we can see how the buildings themselves are shaped by the city-territory as they exhibit a variety of surfaces, stairways, heights, slopes, terraces, canals, gardens, fields, and long, straight, or curved routes; these are complex, changeable forms that we encounter in segments as we cross the city. The body adapts to these changes and is moulded by these material structures, which, in turn, are built in relation to the body. This is as true for the ancient city as it is for the modern one. Today, however, people move less on foot and more by car, motorcycle, or public transit. We are dealing with bodies in motion on banal, flat, or cubic forms, be they functional or bizarre – bodies that travel through the city in both real and (once again) symbolic terms. In this activity of the body, psychology conditions the physiognomy, while architecture functions as living thought that adapts to and sculpts nature itself into a profusion of forms. For human beings, this is similar to flying, falling, gliding, or stopping in front of a blind wall as though we were reading the intricate map of possible itineraries available in the metropolis.

But what do the urban territory and human population that has settled there look like today? If we think of the city as transparent shells, we have before us the image of swirls, such as we might find in a science fiction film: swarms of people forming swaths of living and pulsating matter on the earth. Dense groups of beings move in unison and push one another from one position or recess to another with similar, different, or variable speeds, multiplying to create new colonies in a pulsating, feverish appropriation of the globe. The density of the colonies expanding on the earth provides an image of the human race and its biological urge to settle and operate in an infinite number of communities, where it can take hold, slip, spread, and migrate. In a symbolic image of today's condition, it is possible to capture the difference between what there was before the city and what occurs after the city:

> With cities, it is as with dreams: everything imaginable can be dreamed, but even the most unexpected dream is a rebus that conceals a desire or, its reverse, a fear. Cities, like dreams, are made of desires and fears, even if the thread of their discourse is secret, their rules are absurd, their perspectives deceitful, and everything conceals something else. (Calvino 1974, 51)

THE FORMS OF THE CITY

A form is a whole whose parts are not simply connected by jux-taposition and contiguity; they obey an intrinsic law, the only one capable of determining the meaning of the parts as taken together. I am referring to the forms of the city, taking as my starting point the gaze and the act of observing, which places figures against a background and at the same time captures the field of perception as a dynamic whole. Here, figures are perceived on the basis of their appearance, proximity, symmetry, immobility, or direction of motion. We inherit from Plato and Aristotle the fact that the problem of form is not distinguishable in absolute terms from essence. In my study, however, I follow the interpretation provided by Henri Focillon (1987, 4–5) who, quoting Honoré de Balzac, states that everything is form; life itself is form. It is not an outline, a profile, or a contingency, but an expression of the living world. If we think of art, that is, painting and architecture, the formal relationships within an artwork must occupy space for the artwork to exist. Focillon (ibid., 26) adds that forms are not reducible to the schema or skeleton of representation. Their life comes into being in the material changes in quality brought about by the instruments and the work of human beings. Forms come into existence in a space that is not the abstract square of geometry. They exist in a very concrete and differentiated world. It is in light of this enormous variety of techniques applied throughout the history of an artwork that we can see how every reproduction is an active, rather than a passive, one. On the basis of this principle, our gaze perceives the city by reading, and thus comparing, not its existing forms as much as its living forms.

Archival documents, maps, drawings, stories, photos, and various iconographies provide us with images of the city, from the Roman mosaics of the *Liber Floridus* (1120), an illustrated manuscript by Lambert, Canon of Saint-Omer; to Giotto's fresco *Exorcism of the Demons at Arezzo* (late 1200s to early 1300s); to Taddeo di Bartolo's wooden altarpiece in which Saint Antilla holds up a model of the city of Montepulciano, and Ambrogio Lorenzetti's frescos *Allegory of Good Government* and *Effects of Good Government in the City* (1338 to 1339). These are a few of the countless images of ancient cities and, subsequently, of modern ones. We enjoy wandering through archaeological sites dreaming of imaginary architectural forms that correspond roughly to those that actually existed at one time. The forms we evoke become confused with those of possible reconstructions as we enter the realm of history through the experience of encountering ruins. Many examples flood our minds depending on the trips we take in reality or in the imagination: Hittite, Babylonian, Etruscan, Greek, and Roman cities, as well as those that were founded later in different parts of the world, including, naturally, Athens, Rome, Carthage, Constantinople, and many others located in all four corners of the globe.

As the site of a cohesive community, be it large or small, the city represents an increasingly complex form of human organization: a fabric of public and private buildings, roads, neighbourhoods, squares, stadiums, and gateways through which traffic passes. The division of the city into districts (residential, commercial, administrative, and industrial) today seems to be disappearing as a result of the expansion of built-up areas that mix functions and activities, thereby creating vast homologizing urban zones. In conjunction with this physical expansion, there is the temporal stratification of historic sites with identifiable periods and architectural styles. Different ruins accumulate over the same location. Works of restoration bring before our eyes a sensibility and intelligence, and the value of remembrance, and thus produce a system of cultural and artistic identity. Ancient traces and ruins become enveloped by an aura of nostalgia, starting with Diderot, but the aesthetic and ethical question these ruins pose is itself an ancient one. In the famous letter that Servius Sulpicius Rufus sent in 45 BCE to Cicero, his mentor and friend, to console him for the loss of his daughter Tullia (*Epistulae ad familiares* [*Letters to His Friends*], 8, book 4, 5), Rufus describes his return from Asia, during which he saw cities that once flourished but were now destroyed and abandoned. In this letter of condolence, he reflects on the pointlessness of sorrow caused by the awareness of the brevity of life, as opposed to that caused by the destruction of cities that often were meant to last forever by those who designed them.

For the most part, cities are laid out in a checkerboard or radial pattern, both with variants. Traditionally in China and in the United States, the first applies, whereas in Europe we find an orthogonal city grid laid over a Roman system. In other instances, the urban development is axial, that is, when the expansion is linear. Whether designed like a broad network or one that converges on a central point, the city has a thousand forms as determined by the cultures that represent it and the tastes of the peoples who emerge in the course of human history. Renaissance urban planning, with such a famous work as Palmanova in northeastern Italy, produced toward the end of the 1500s, revived the radial plan, likely introduced by Piero della Francesca in his *The Ideal City* (1480–1490). Conceived to give an orderly and rational form to the city, the radial design with point symmetry was introduced in the projects of Leon Battista Alberti, Filarete's drawing of the plan for Sforzinda, and Francesco di Giorgio Martini's fortified cities: ideal geometric forms later adopted by Sebastiano Serlio, Andrea Palladio, and Vincenzo Scamozzi. One has only to enter the Teatro Olimpico (Olympic Theatre) in Vicenza to experience directly this visual and spatial strategy.

In a broader historical context, we find the city types that appeared along the Euphrates, Tigris, and Indus rivers. Through imagined reconstructions of these cities, we come to understand the history and customs of entire populations. My own passion, however, is for ancient Greece, beyond the charm that I experience strolling through the ruins of Mycenae, Miletus, and Delphi. Unlike the "palace cities" built in Mesopotamia, the Greek civilization created city fortresses, adopting a spatial strategy that separated the *agora* from the acropolis, plain from plateau – a model that recurs repeatedly throughout the Mediterranean.

In the fifth century BCE, Hippadamus of Miletus, an architect and collaborator of Pericles, designed an ideal city for 10,000 people that accommodated three social classes: peasants, crafts-men, and warriors. It was divided into quarters and had a plani-metric layout, a design that was probably already in use during his lifetime, though not systematically. Main and secondary roads divided the space into regular square blocks or long strips. We find the layout of Miletus and Cyrene in Priene, Corinth, Ephesus, and elsewhere. The beautiful city of Pergamon was arranged to produce a scenographic effect for the display of its monuments, using a model that is noted in particular for its library. As new visitors and admirers of picturesque ancient Greece, we travel among the places of history with Pausanias as our guide from the second century CE. Many centuries have passed, but the spirit of the places seems to live again in his passages. We can perhaps also taste the sweetness of life that inspired the Greeks to enjoy the pleasures of the banquet and the symposium, as well as to appreciate the symbolic and social functions of their eating practices. In some places, the cities still display traces of the aspect of their character that led to places in which to meet and to converse, as well as spaces for participating in the community's culture and rituals, or the co-citizenship of humans and gods. We find these existing next to one another in the public area of the *polis*, in the market, porticos, houses, and sacred dwellings, while the statues arrayed along the roads speak to us of the symbolic value of myths. We might recall that Plato told the story of a friendship between the gods and humans (*Symposium*, 188c). As we imagine hearing great orators in the *agora*, we observe, among the ruins, examples and fragments of a Greek culture destroyed by time and human actions; fragments of Doric, Ionic, and Corinthian architectural orders lie on the ground: ideas outside of history, silent emblems of a civilization that has come to an end. And from a ship leaving the port of a Greek city sailing for Rome, during the reign of Tiberius, a cry can be heard: according to Plutarch, "The great Pan is dead" (as he writes in *On the Failure of Oracles*).

From Athens we move to Rome, the new capital of power and culture in the Mediterranean, which we recall with pride as we gaze at its ruins. As the saying goes, *Roma quanta fuit, ipsa ruina docet* (How great Rome was, its very ruins tell). The saying, attributed to Hildebert of Lavardin (1055–1133), bishop of Le Mans and archbishop of Tours, is relevant here and suggests a comprehensive image of the collapse of Rome in the centuries following the sack of the city at the hands of the Goths in 410 CE. Great works destined to last forever begin to lie in the dust, enveloped by vegetation. The fall of Rome becomes increasingly evident with the abandonment of houses and public works that are no longer maintained, along with the progressive loss of knowledge and skills. In order to decentralize imperial power, Ravenna and Milan are given increasing importance in the second half of the first millennium. The capital becomes progressively poorer and the aristocrats withdraw to the countryside. But what was ancient imperial Rome like? Since we have many resources that enable us to form an understanding of the way it was, I will not describe here the styles and cults that prevailed up to the rise of Christianity. We can easily find models of the Roman house and plans of the ancient Roman city. I will make only a brief remark to say that, as Paul Zanker illustrates, Rome was founded in the seventh century BCE, and developed at a wide bend in the Tiber river, where the Via Sacra, which runs from the Palatine to the Capitoline hill and passes through the Roman Forum, plays an important role. The area facing the port, as well as the bridges spanning the river, has constituted the centre of the public space for a millennium. Along this strip, which extends on each side to form an orthogonal grid developed along the axes of the *cardo* and the *decumanus*, temples and public buildings were constructed by successive emperors and were imitated in the colonial cities from Britannia to the Mediterranean coastline of Africa. The forum, within which we find temples, the curia, the *comitium*, basilicas, the theatre, the arena, thermal baths, and the circus, represented urbanized territory. The city was connected to the colonies by consular roads, such as the Appian, Flaminian, Aurelian, and Emilian, both sides of which were subdivided into lots along flat terrains, applying a method of land measurement known as centuriation. Along these arteries the capital city transported its aesthetic models and its power.

The houses of the wealthy (*domus*) were luxurious, with opulent gardens, situated next to the houses of the poor (*tabernae*). The shrines were grandiose and were designed to inspire awe in visitors. Two examples are the Sanctuary of Fortuna Primigenia in Palestrina and the Sanctuary of Hercules at Tivoli, both of which are located on mountain slopes, creating spectacular visual effects. In the first case, the architect, perhaps influenced by Hellenistic buildings in the east, revived the sacred buildings of the past, adding a panoramic view by constructing a symmetrical system of terraces. From this elevated position, the pilgrim could enjoy a splendid view of the valley and the Colli Albani (Alban Hills) after prayers or during a theatrical performance. Landscape and architecture were integrated to produce a sense of unity. A similar effect was achieved at Tivoli, with its superimposed arcades and porticos, adapted to conform to the uneven terrain. The thermal baths of Caracalla and Diocletian were massive. They were not built solely for the care of the body but were true recreation centres. The swimming pools, courtyards, gymnasiums, gardens, halls for orators, and libraries were designed for pleasure and leisure. The emperors tried to outdo one another in splendour, both in Rome and in their country residences. We need only think of Hadrian's Villa at Tivoli, with its emphasis on celebrating different cults and its tribute to the philosophers; it was constructed on a site that had been used earlier, in the Republican age. We also have the Colosseum of the Flavians, the most perfect and grandiose amphitheatre of its time. This self-celebration was evident to visitors even before they entered the city, from outside the city walls, where there were funerary monuments and triumphal arches erected to honour the emperors. Rome was adopted as a model for the various cities of the empire, and the original conformity to the model slowly gave way to formal modifications according to the areas, geography, and functions.

Something that occurs less frequently, but is very useful to this study, is the relationship between the city and its natural surroundings, such as that among the home, garden, and land-scape. Through the study of the relationship between interior and exterior elements, we can better understand the lifestyle of those who lived in ancient Rome. To go out of the city, walk through the burial sites of different religious cults, into the gardens, through cultivated fields, pastures, and woods, and stay in a villa, represents a key aspect of Roman culture. It is an interesting aspect we can experience by reading some of Pliny the Younger's letters. But what is most fascinating is the fresco in Villa of Livia that depicts the way the Romans saw and imagined their home, their town, and the natural world outside the home and garden. What is involved is a play of gazes examining the environment, which we sense is still close to us in some way.

Christianity, with its basilicas, changed the appearance of the city. For Chiara Frugoni (1983, 31), Rome transforms the myth of empire into that of spiritual magisterium. What is more, the crisis of power, coinciding with the frequent invasions and raids, compels the aristocracy to withdraw to other cities or to the countryside, where rural dwellings are reinforced with defensive structures to become fortified towns with towers and solid walls. Over the decades, with the disappearance of specialized skills and the scarcity of economic resources, a custom developed of using materials from pagan Roman buildings for new constructions. But what is the city at the end of the empire? Augustine and Isidorus underscore the two concepts that prevail until the pre-commune age: *urbs* and *civitas*, that is, the "stones" of the city and the citizens. In Christian symbolism, the city is supposed to provide religious protection and refuge. Gregory the Great, in his *Homiliae in Evangelia* (*Homilies on the Gospels*), describes the city as a great house in which one can feel safe, a *domus panis* (house of bread), with a clear Christological reference, and identifies it with Bethlehem. How are *urbs* and *civitas* reflected in the layout of the city? The answer is: in the circle, which can be either empty or filled with symbolic holy figures.

According to Frugoni (ibid., 11), up to the end of the first millennium, the city is represented either as a circle of walls with towers or a large embracing belt, expressing the only feeling that it seems to have inspired in its inhabitants: a sense of refuge and protection. Even the Earthly Paradise assumes the form of a city. In those centuries, men and women saw themselves as Adam and Eve, who had to go outside of the walls, defenseless, in order to face the vast world, which had become hostile as a consequence of the biblical curse. The journey is one of separation and anguish.

As Laura Falqui tells us, among the many forms of cities in history, there are also imagined cities created in literature: orthogonal, crystalline, circular, labyrinthine, metamorphic, and arborescent ones. They are ethereal, oneiric, or disquieting because they are evoked by words, either following tradition or using the free imagination. Those inspired by tradition include John of Patmos's New Jerusalem, while those produced by the imagination include Arthur C. Clarke's Lys (from *The City and the Stars*). The first is the city of God, the architect of the universe, which descends from the heavens. Its proportions are enormous; its walls are high and have twelve gates. It is made of precious stone and stands as a shining example of the perfection of the heavens. The square before it appears to be of pure gold and clear glass; the base is made of jasper, sapphire, chalcedony, emerald, sardonyx, chrysolite, beryl, topaz, agate, yellow zircon, and amethyst. Rescued from the desert and technology, Lys has, instead, tree-lined streets, which are described as streams of perfumes and scents: the senses bloom like flowers. The buildings are architecturally complex and ornamented. There is a giant pointed arch below which we see clearings, woods, and streams. Lys and Nowhere are within us. We have internal cities, the products of our dreams, as well as cities such as Angkor Wat that reflect the order of the heavens, utopian cities like Thomas More's, and cities of serenity like Shangri-La. Cities of joy, and cities of sorrow. In the prism of the imagination and emotions, there are countless images and features.

Novels have described cities exhaustively. We read them in order to live in the story and to admire the complexity and variety of the architecture in the same way that we are in awe of nature. In general, from a very long potential list, we can mention the Paris of Boileau, Balzac, and Baudelaire; the London of Dickens; the Milan of Manzoni; the Rome of D'Annunzio; the Turin of Nietzsche; the Prague of Kafka; the Venice of Ruskin; the Berlin of Benjamin; and the Algiers of Camus. The city often appears as a canvas consisting of clichés and common objects, and it is used as the background for the stories being narrated. This is evident right up to DeLillo's *Cosmopolis*. There are also powerful images, and it is the writers of the 1700s that capture our attention, with their style combining wit and the picturesque, because they offer us a picture of the first true megacities of the age, such as Paris and London. We read descriptions of eighteenth-century Paris in Voltaire, Prévost, and Rétif de la Bretonne, while a delightful, magical reconstruction of that city can be found in Éric Rohmer's film *The Lady and the Duke* (2001). London is depicted by John Gay in *Trivia*, which shows us how to move in the new urban spaces, while a reconstruction of that city from a woman's perspective is available in the works of Charlotte Lennox and Frances Burney. As Franco Moretti has argued (1987, § 138), the novel has shaped the character of the urban habitat. We owe our expanded knowledge of contemporary life in the city to writers as well as film directors. It is they who discovered the grandeur and beauty of those places, through which ordinary people pass without being aware of that beauty. With sensitivity, they have created a sense of the space being portrayed, transforming it into a landscape of mobility. Time is compressed into space, and space expands into time.

In centuries past, people would go outside the city walls to stroll through the fields, walk barefoot on the grass, follow a stream, and enjoy the experience, as we read in Plato's *Phaedrus*. Nowadays, we can sometimes feel unsure if we are still on earth or are actors in a science fiction film when we arrive in cities like Dubai, Singapore, Hong Kong, or Shanghai: postmodern, generic, and shocking cities that have become the legacy not so much of culture as of indifference. The mix of a distant past and a present lived as if it were already the future can make us feel like consumers. We consume images even when, as enlightened tourists or amateur archaeologists, we contemplate works executed in the Moghul style in a ghost city like Fatehpur Sikri, built in the Uttar Pradesh state in northern India by the Moghul emperor Akbar between 1570 and 1573, and abandoned a short time later. We consume images when, with exhilaration, we cross Central Park or the most attractive streets and squares of New York, as well as other megacities. These are enchanted cities. We consume images when we observe certain areas of cities by night or during the summer. These are empty cities. We also consume images when we look at the skeletons of bombed out cities, which we visit after the end of terrible conflicts. These are dead cities. Such images resonate with the most joyful and the most sorrowful part of our being. We can see ourselves as protagonists in the film *The Truman Show*. What is artificial and what is genuine in our joy and our sadness? Interweaving the ancient and the modern, the forms evoke richly nuanced atmospheres and impressions: we intuit the spirit of the city in which we move. The forms relate to the styles, and the styles, in turn, suggest segregation. Think of the European quarters in the cities of the so-called colonies or the ghettos scattered across the globe. Where are we? Can we still recognize ourselves? Our identity blurs and we are no longer in familiar surroundings, and yet we are still capable of participating in a new social setting with different peoples.

To conclude this portion of the chapter, I would like to point out that, in the age of globalization, borders become increasingly hazy, remote, and indistinct as agricultural land is devoured, and wrapped in menacing smog. These are the features of the territorial habitat. Some are of the opinion that this will signal the end of the city as civilization is accelerated by these phenomena. According to Oswald Spengler, the decline of the West and the city, as both a real and a symbolic entity, as I have attempted to explain in the preceding pages, is being exacerbated by great transformations, which are causing a loss of meaning, both explicit and implicit, of the city's features, located symbolically in the natural environment. Along with the forms, living beings too are losing their defining characteristics. Although this may be so, we can also interpret the changes differently and see in European cities a tangible inversion, in the eco-consciousness and green architecture of recent years. These give us reason for hope in humankind and the dignity of its history. I wish to underscore Henri Lefebvre's view (1976, 71) that the city is a work of art. This is because urban areas are not only planned and constructed, they are also shaped, adapted, and made their own by various social groups in accordance with their needs, aesthetics, ethics, and ideology.

THE SEDUCTION OF ANTIQUITY

To this point, I have discussed forms, but I attributed to them the feelings and moods that are always present when we approach an object from an aesthetic perspective. In a broad overview of the quality of building and living practices, we can also identify the desire to relive the atmosphere of a town in a different and distant land. This is true of the ethnic enclaves of the cities of the West, as well as those of cities in Africa, Asia, and India. This desire can exist even if the place of origin has very different social conditions (such as totalitarianism imposed by various colonialist or imperialist powers upon the occupied territories). We find examples of English Neo-Gothic in India, late Manuelin in Africa, Ottoman architecture in Greece and in Arab countries, and so on. These stylistic features are also affected by the experiences of the cities' inhabitants; people mould their natural surroundings. The house is the entire world for those who live in it. In houses, boroughs, and neighbourhoods, we find both individual and collective identity. As Marco Romano (1993, 271) points out, each house expresses in a recognizable fashion and at every moment the way each individual adapts to the continually changing form of the ideal. Within a given local community, we encounter a system of conventions and customs that become part of the physical aspect of the house (as determined by the relationships of cohabitation). In the same place, we find variations in taste that comprise the style of an area or a neighbourhood of the city linked to that particular social group.

The city has always attracted and seduced us. Above all, we are susceptible to the aura of antiquity in its different layers, even though we have been experiencing a crisis of urban beauty in recent decades. Increasingly and in dramatic fashion, we are witnessing a rapid decline in the fascination with metropoli, at least the historic ones. When he described Paris shortly after the mid-1930s, Roger Caillois understood it as a modern myth, created by the splendid pages of a literature that reflected the life and development of the city. In this century, however, the imagination of the *flâneurs* and the correspondence between the visions of solitary *promeneurs* (walkers) and styles of architecture seem to have disappeared. This sensibility, which was expressed in modernist taste, has diminished in recent years as Paris, with the exception of the historic-monumental area, has come under the spell of postmodernism – though not to the extent of London, which is well on its way to losing its traditional character. The negative aspect of the radical change does not come from the work of a few "starchitects," whose works are certainly admirable, if somewhat outlandish, from Renzo Piano's Shard to Norman Foster's Gherkin. The architectural transformation becomes painful as a result of the mediocre inventiveness of engineers and architects who have adapted to the competition spurred by real estate speculation. Architectural genius has lost its true mission.

We see *kitsch* everywhere, together with the loss of beauty. The historic cities, however, continue to make efforts to preserve the aura of the past: myths that survive alongside new myths that remind us of the observations of Roland Barthes (1967) in one respect and those of Paul Virilio (2004; 2011) in another. The latter, in particular, provides the reader a study of the current dematerialization of the gaze, the decline of the art of seeing and representing, as it has unfolded recently in the artistic realm. The system of totalizing computerization has either paralyzed or erased the real by promoting the virtual, given the ubiquity of media. According to this line of thinking, society has de-realized the world, and as a result the city, with its complexity and identity. Still, pollution, overcrowding, and issues relating to mobility remain real for millions of inhabitants of the metropolis. Hyper-reality coexists strangely with the concrete problems of daily life; globalization has ushered in a new level of urban density that enhances the city's representations and myths. As Rykwert explains (2002), the city is a precious and inalienable part of human achievement. It must be considered a legacy of the actions of living, inhabiting, and communicating. Perhaps we need to rethink Thomas More's *Utopia* or Tommaso Campanella's *La città del sole* (*City of the Sun*), as well as experimental garden cities, and Paolo Soleri's most recent works. Today the megacity is perhaps the magnified modern version of the "world city" that Fernand Braudel studied, a city of markets, financial power, and commerce.

In the first years of the third millennium, we still find ourselves talking about contemplation of beautiful things, landscape, and the city. When we travel, we find ourselves enveloped by what seems to be a gentle, seductive fascination as we admire the forms of ancient architecture. But it becomes vertigo, as Jean Baudrillard might say, when we allow our gaze to be attracted by the hybrid forms of modern architecture through the power of the media. We experience real emotion in visiting archaeological parks and imagining cities of the past, just as we experience dizziness in the presence of postmodern and neo-modern eccentricities. With respect to ancient cities, there is a valorization of the object, which evokes a feeling of nostalgia and emotional involvement. This is the rhetorical modality of the gaze before objects that are present (material) and objects that are absent (virtual substitutes for the real), unfolding on a number of fronts.

But what is the aesthetic of the ancient city? Antiquity stimulates the sense of the beautiful as a remote, profound feeling for life, objects, and nature in its various manifestations, as well as for artifacts and materials. Feeling springs from the simple act of perceiving. In fact, aesthetics originally referred to the domain of sensations and emotions; in philosophical discourse, the term *aesthesis* is used around the fifth century CE to refer to characteristics of beauty and grace. At the moment of perceiving an aesthetic quality, time is suspended and the impression is crystallized, becoming a perception that emphasizes a sense of belonging to the earth, the community, and the divine. Beauty is joined to what is good, and to doing things well, through combining aesthetics and ethics. At the same time, although philosophical reflection introduces the idea of *logos*, Greek culture valorizes the condition of wonder in those who observe nature. Thus is born in the West an aesthetic feeling that accompanies reflecting on an object, a statement of principles, and an articulation of artistic canons. In this way, aesthetics injects a certain distance or theoretical detachment into the vision. This dual nature has persisted for more than twenty centuries, up to our own times. When in Europe we speak of an aesthetics of the city, we are referring to the fascination with the past, which emanates from architectural forms and their location, combining with both our evaluation of these forms and the pleasure they generate in our imagination. Our mind sees with the instruments of archaeology and history, but contemplates the symbols of myth and culture in affirming an inner vision. The desire to understand a past world combines with an imagined reconstruction of that world. This is active contemplation, because it involves effort exerted in the study of the object we have before us; after the statue, painting, mosaic, amphora, jewel, and architectural structure, the city as a whole also becomes the object of our attention. We produce an aesthetic synthesis of the city by fusing the objective data with the data of subjective knowledge, memory, and imagination. When I speak of the value of conserving nature, art, culture, and civilization as the heritage of humanity, I am saying that there is a coalescing of feeling and form, wherein aesthetics and ethics, the beauty that is to be preserved, and the actions undertaken to conserve it, coincide. This is because beauty is not something superficial; it is not a means for improving the appearance of things. It is, instead, linked closely to human activity and the options available for that activity. It is a constitutive element of culture and civilization. It is variable, not homogeneous, and subject to change.

It is evident that the city is not a closed entity but a variable and heterogeneous one, and yet it expresses an identity, albeit a composite one. For Romano, the continuous search for the *civitas* can be found in a physical form that acquires a succession of styles reflecting the will of the collectivity that promotes it. A single style or an array of styles, from private or public palaces to religious or popular houses, becomes visible in the form of the city as the product of the deliberations of groups, and of the creative intentionality of artists. The will of the *civitas* is expressed in the stylistic rhythm of the architecture of the *urbs*. It is the form of the *urbs* itself that suggests or ties into each successive modification and raises the question of visual coherence. Rodulfus Glaber (in the first decades of the year 1000), Thomas Aquinas, Dino Compagni (in the mid-1300s), Leon Battista Alberti and Filarete (in the 1400s), and later Vincenzo Scamozzi and others raise the issue of the appearance of buildings, the façades of houses, and the physiognomy of roads, thereby initiating a conversation on the question of the aesthetics of the city – the organic features of its identity relative to the surrounding territory, involving a web of symbols, metaphors, and other figures, such as we find in the rhetoric.

I would like to emphasize the attraction of place as the site of living and being, of acting and of experiencing pleasure in one's life.

From its origins, the city has been the principal method of organization and representation of space, adhering to social and ideal norms. Architectural and urban structures correspond to cultural domains or to the more abstract areas of philosophy. Form is not separate from content: lines, colours, lights, solids, and surfaces disclose a meaning that goes beyond appearance. It contends that there exists a formal analogy between Medieval scholasticism and cathedrals in that both are intelligible systems constructed using identical methods, including, among other things, a rigorous separation of their constituent parts and absolute clarity of the formal hierarchies in the harmonization of opposites. During the Renaissance, geometry, perspective, and mathematical order combined with the new demands of communication and military art. Ideal cities, irrespective of their geometric order, are closed spaces. Later, open spaces prevailed, and the image changed to become a field of forces characterized by functions and movements.

Today, Medieval, Renaissance, and baroque cities provide us with a comforting human reality in whose architectural forms we can immerse ourselves. They are a refuge in the face of the devastating power of the new urban settlements and suburbs. The city reflects the values of a society. Like a biological organism, the nucleus of the city can undergo a series of rapid changes determined by chaos and necessity, as biologists would say. In any century, a social change can ascribe a fixed form to the lengthy period that follows. As Romano claims, the ancient city, with its temples, theatres, squares, and gymnasiums, lasted a thousand years prior to the Common Era, just as the modern European city has, from the time of its establishment around the year 1000 CE to the present day. As has happened in the past and is happening in the present, continual change has modified a city template that once seemed immutable.

To inhabit a city aesthetically means to understand its visible and structural features: the opening of rooms onto a patio or street, the vertical and horizontal extension of buildings and the groups that they form, the pattern of the streets and squares corresponding to the dynamics of sensibility and form. There is a distinct relationship between the distribution of structures and materials, and the spirit of storytelling, which has always been a feature of the human adventure. We can consider the city as a text made of stones, a graphic invention, and a fabric made of symbols and meanings with grammatical and syntactical elements, representing a rhetoric of space enlivened by recurring figures.

There are ideal labyrinths in which to move. I am thinking of the importance of strolling through the city or the countryside. In the hybrid city, there are no places that we can really call gardens or lanes, capable of demonstrating the art of organizing rural and urban spaces. So many writers have written about the pleasure of walking, an activity that is now deadened by traffic. Since antiquity, walking has been one of the highest expressions of taste. Philosophy, the garden, the city, and nature are the foundation of our civilizations. To observe with our dynamic synesthetic perception, with the flow of the senses driven by the natural rhythm of the things around us, means rediscovering our most intimate and human capacity for feeling, and to do so without incongruous buildings clashing with the methods of construction that have been around for centuries (in terms of materials, colours, measurements, and so on), or industrial plants and cables intruding to spoil the experience.

For some time now we have been witnessing the fraying of the dignity of the city, the memory of whose past is declining inexorably.

At this point I would like to cite an example that foregrounds a disturbing aspect of the issue being discussed here. I have in mind not a vista or point of view where the position of the observer is fixed, but rather a mobile gaze, that is, the eye that moves about and admires the cityscape. We could say that there are cities in which the eye encounters a system of vertical views, as in Bologna or Venice, and cities like Rome where the gaze glides horizontally, like a wide-angle lens. In recent years, well-known archaeological research has been conducted on the Palatine hill, examining the viewpoint desired by the emperors, from which to enjoy the sight of the city. In the capital, however, efforts to renew this ancient gaze have come at a cost in terms of the enormous degradation and damage done to the historical-architectural legacy. During the Fascist era, this occurred with the demolition carried out in order to build the Via della Conciliazione, which runs directly into St Peter's. For this project the fabric of small, pre-existing buildings in the area around the Basilica was destroyed. This was also the case with the excavations made for the Via dei Fori Imperiali, which cuts through the buildings in the area and connects the Colosseum with Piazza Venezia, carving out in the process a telescopic perspective, in a zone that is perhaps the richest in the world in terms of monuments and other traces of the past. In terms of its complexity and multiformity, the aesthetics of the ancient city is, in a sense, humiliated through the loss of large sections of its memory. The vista, which is now modern with buildings designed in the Littorio style built along this immense wound inflicted on the land and on its history, is praised nonetheless. It was a useful artifice in the rhetoric of the regime of the 1920s and 1930s, that is, in the language of totalitarian power. After years of continuous archaeological excavation in that area, the eye can now enjoy, despite the disaster, a greater number of monuments representing different historical periods, styles, and methods of construction. What is evident here is an expansive and horizontal aesthetic power of the gaze that allows us to meditate on a monstrous paradox: the spirit of the ancient past is nourished by the sacrifice of that same antiquity, an artistic patrimony deposited through the centuries. The demolition of buildings from the Middle Ages and other time periods is counterbalanced by the valorization of other aspects that have come to light and offer themselves for viewing. We have the option of moving quickly or slowly among the epochs and historical legacy in a panorama where the eye can either linger on or disregard the disruption of those forms.

And what can we say about the new urban territory? We have discussed spaces, but it would be preferable to talk about places. As Rykwert has affirmed, we need to reconsider the way we think about building activity and its objectives using different terms:

> We can no longer afford to read the city as an amorphous stringing out along freeways into conurbations as futurologists once did. The city can be understood only in the context of its landscape, as part of its inalienable region, but also as an entity with one or more designated centres, with marked edges – if only on the map. (2000, 224)

Architects must pursue a responsible action plan that gives legible form to building projects and controls the figurative potential of the forms they develop. Urban planning and building should be thought of as political acts and should create places, and not spaces whose meaning illustrates the limitations of abstract geometric design. It is necessary to provide designated areas that citizens can inhabit and make their own without jarring contrasts, always keeping in mind the interconnected objects made by people, objects that form the fabric of a place. Rykwert (ibid., 307) goes on to say that to mould the city and allow it to become the expression of its citizens, the ongoing participation or involvement of the community is indispensable. To properly construct the fabric of the territorial habitat, we must conduct a study of humankind in order to understand the way human experience converts constructed forms into images. The architect should endeavour to bring people and projects together and should take concrete steps to make this happen, as we see in the works of Kazuyo Sejima. I would like to mention just one of these, the 21st Century Museum of Contemporary Art in Kanazawa, Japan. Here, spaces have become places where visitors enter and leave without encountering any obstacles as they experience the lightness and transparency of the building and its light, as well as where the surroundings are transformed into harmonious structures (or forms) as the visitor passes through the galleries. The gaze that moves without encountering any obstructions is drawn upward, where it does not find a ceiling and can touch the sky. Sejima would have pleased Derrida because the architect is both a deconstructionist and at the same time a re-constructionist whose works do not exhibit the slightest effort in achieving this effect.

This is a museum, but a museum is also part of the place where people live, and it puts on display works of visual and plastic art, exhibits, and events. Collections are becoming of secondary importance; culture is becoming a mass spectacle. It is representative of power; it is a meeting place with science fiction-inspired buildings designed by contemporary "starchitects." This is true of the MOMA in New York and the Guggenheim Bilbao Museum, as well as the new exposition sites in Doha, Dubai, Abu Dhabi, and Beijing. Museums constructed around the world in the last few years compete in scale with modern stadiums or the ancient thermal baths so as to become like new *agoras*.

THE NATURE OF THE URBAN LANDSCAPE

What is the nature of the city? We see its physical aspect in stone, wood, brick, and cement. Yet the forms that hold the city together like the ties that bind, though nowadays frayed in several points, suggest an existence produced and conditioned by an irrepressible internal energy. What, then, is its nature? It is a state or condition that propagates on the basis of a more general *poiesis* or creativity associated with ceaseless human productivity. This poetic idea and this energy, which permeate the organization and assembly of material objects, are captured in Spinoza's expression *natura naturans, natura naturata* (naturing nature, natured nature) (*Ethics* I, 29) and Vincent of Beauvais's *Speculum Maius* (*The Great Mirror*). In the second half of the 1200s, the expression meant the following: "naturing nature" is God as creator and source of all events, and "natured nature" is the totality of things and laws created by Him. For my own purposes, I would prefer to focus on the thinking that comes after Bacon (*Novum Organum* II, 1) (*The New Organon*), which interprets the terms more concretely, wherein *natura naturans* is the disposition or process that manifests itself to our senses as an aspect of a perceived quality, which is to say, nature. In this interpretation, the famous phrase *natura naturans, natura naturata* could be considered synonymous with form, a form that connotes an essence in experience.

As we have seen in the preceding pages, in order to inhabit the earth, humans dug furrows and divided the land to correspond to the signs they saw in the sky and the movements of the stars. Rising from the land are cities, *urbes*, a term similar to *urvae*, which are trenches made by a plough as it carves the fields. Because of this, the city does not appear only as the blood-stained place of desperation, but also as a fertile area of hope offered by art, which is to say, by a specific technique or practice that gives meaning to things and establishes human order among those things. To achieve this, attention must be paid to small things without indulging consumerism, formalism, or utilitarianism, but rather good living. In this sense, inhabited land is a place we must safeguard. These are the small things to which the expression *natura naturans* refers.

We can frame the question of the nature of the urban landscape more precisely by citing the viewpoint expressed by Mikel Dufrenne in the early 1930s. His is an extremely apt interpretation, to my mind. Dufrenne reads the Latin phrase in a non-metaphysical way, since humans and nature appear to be both joined and apart at the same time. In such a relationship of similarity and difference between object and subject, he asserts, if we did not have the image of *homo artifex* (man the artisan), that is, humans intervening in the world with their work, by the same token we would not have the image of *natura artifex* (nature the artisan), which would exclude humans completely. As we know, nature is a product of culture and history. In light of the foregoing remarks, nature appears to be the interaction between the natural and the artificial, nature and art, which manages to integrate post-industrial architecture into the urban landscape; what is seen as not natural, once its technical and social function is exhausted, is reabsorbed into the aesthetic paradigms of the urban landscape. From this perspective, nature seems to be nurturing humankind, both the artists who transfigure nature and the consumers/observers who lose themselves in the appreciation or contemplation of the work. They discover nature within themselves, that is, the original and spontaneous core that becomes the world.

The expression *natura naturans, natura naturata* is historically at the centre of the question of imitation, truth, and artifice. By imitating nature, art acts as a naturing agent through the genius that nature infuses in people. And when we speak of natured, we are referring to what is inherent in our awareness of the world that belongs to us. We recall the words of Immanuel Kant:

Independent natural beauty reveals to us a technic of nature that allows us to present nature as a system in terms of laws

whose principle we do not find anywhere in our understanding: the principle of a purposiveness directed to our
use of judgment as regards appearances. Under this principle, appearances must be judged as belonging not merely
to nature as governed by its purposeless mechanism, but
also to [nature considered by] analogy with art. (1987, 99)

According to Dufrenne, in the wake of Kant and Simmel, it is
up to humankind to experience nature as the world and to actu-
alize the possibilities that lie within the real. In this sense,
humankind itself is both nature and creative potential. Nature,
art, and culture are interconnected. Humankind is at the centre
of this double concept. Dufrenne writes: "Whether we are dealing with the work itself, the praxis of the artist, or the aura of the
perceived object, we intuit everywhere the *poiesis* of Nature …
How can we refuse to contemplate this tireless presence of the
magma from which we are born and to which the experience of
art continues to bear witness?" (1981, 48).

In the early 1990s, Marc Augé developed this theme in particular with his notion of "non-place"; however, he describes
the opposite, which is to say, the vacuum of identity of many
modern buildings (emporia, shops, airports, etc.). Essentially,
he sees an enormous waste of human energy that is a natural
part of the *poiesis* or creativity of the previous few years, and he
does not find that this is caused by the progress or the spirit of
the typical city. The non-place represents an anthropological
landscape where mass culture transforms humanity into a consumer species.

Between the positions of Dufrenne and Augé, we also find
the decline of that taste that for centuries produced an aesthetics of landscape. The theory of the gaze, based on precise modal-
ities of seeing (the belvedere, the frame, and the vista), brings
the natural and the urban into the domain of the visual and
plastic arts, such as painting, photography, and cinema. The crisis of that aesthetic theory leads to a crisis of the entire system
of representation and the feelings associated with it. If we place
ourselves between the two, we find the decline of the pic-

turesque and the advance of a philosophy of design, but not one inspired by utopianism and echoes from the European Renaissance. In assuming this intentionally general position, without suggesting any specific implications for cultural identity, I am taking into account the effect of urbanization and the phenomenon of globalization, and am noting that European culture is vanishing along with its aesthetic values. Coinciding with the disappearance of the Renaissance, baroque, picturesque, and romantic worlds, including their last manifestations in the 1900s, is the rise of a virtual universe in which the images and messages that constantly surround us and imprison our minds generate literally blinding effects. In reality, we see too many things, and in the end it is as if we do not see anything at all. This signals the end of contemplation and of the aura, that of Medieval mystics and of Rousseau, philosopher of nature and solitary wayfarer. From the rubble of European civilization, the smoke rising everywhere, and western artistic civilization is born a new taste: the pleasure that comes from disorientation, the loss of the centre, and the sameness that is the product of globalization. The crisis of the city has led some architects to create material and formal hybrids and to provide eco-friendly consumer products as they push themselves to design vertical gardens; indeed, the bizarre creations of "starchitects" flourish in "non-places." We can find many examples from around the globe. We ignore the concepts of relationship and context, and head straight for the architectural object that stands out above the uniform strata of cement. Today, the "cities" draw to themselves all the resources, both material and intangible, as they now contain half the world's population. This constitutes an enormous risk from an anthropological, political, and aesthetic standpoint. It is as though the geographic distinction between the city and the surrounding natural landscape is dissolving into an ill-defined land waiting to be devoured by the next expanse of asphalt and reinforced concrete.

Thus, the urban landscape finds itself caught between conservation and innovation, principles that we find moving in lock step throughout history. In our times, this war of sorts rarely produces armistices or truces. The great architects of the megacities claim the right to build in the name of the freedom touted by modernism (or postmodernism) and they now want to go into historic cities to deconstruct the system of styles developed over many centuries, because creating a shock effect is their main objective. As well, "recycling," an inventive technique used in both art and architecture, does not eliminate the problem created by an epochal anthropological transformation, which is forced to witness the domination of industry and commerce. Technology seems to prevail and enslave. The dominant *ratio* transforms art and architecture into a parody or a ludic mechanism, and when "recycling" or "slow food" create an alternative system, which is certainly noticeable in social relations, that same rationale subsumes both.

Conservatives, motivated by a sense of adequacy and conformity, in accordance with the principle of relationships and a concept of non-invasive resource exploitation, try to organize the various legacies of history and a culture of landscape, and in the process revive traditional restoration techniques. The cities look out on large natural parks and protected areas. These protected zones will become larger and larger. The new aesthetic forms will flow from the sensibility and corporeality of human nature, which will find solutions that will nearly always be in contradiction to large protected areas on one hand, and megacities on the other. And given the so-called death of art, the process of dissolving the images of the old metropolitan aesthetics through new technologies will also be different. I need to add, however, that for the sake of a hopeful future, there will be large gardens in the cities, combining artificial and natural elements, while the historic cities will try to find harmony in what is increasingly remote, such as the airiness of parks and protected areas, by means of long, green corridors, with the aim of breaking the siege of cement.

Beauty is assuming new forms as artists and philosophers try to make sense of all this. They defend the traditional aesthetic categories even as they work, with irony and playfulness, on virtual reality and signs that are always the same.

I base these reflections on current debates. A questioning gaze is being cast on the expanding city, which seems to be the expression of its internal structure designed to create a relationship with objects on the basis of experience and lived practices. From this emerges the possibility of capturing the spirit of inhabiting and cultivating the land in a manner that takes into account both the city and nature, and adopts principles that pertain to *natura naturans* and *natura naturata*. This point of view is useful for any discussion on the subject, especially today if we take note of the new forms of the city-turned-megacity, beyond any symbolic or metaphoric meaning. What beauty does the inhabited earth have, then? Does it still make sense to speak of beauty? We can study the different places of the world as though the world were an immense sculpture of lines and surfaces in constant change. In considering the cities of the global age, cities of multiple languages, peoples, and modes of communication, from Mexico City and Dubai, to Mumbai and Tokyo, what can we imagine that might exist between "slow cities" and "smart cities"? Slowness, speed, and intelligence intersect to generate possible "aesthetic" solutions to the problem of slowing down or reversing the pace of production or reception, so that technologies can perhaps facilitate the creation of a more human world. In terms of the beauty and the regularity or irregularity of urban landscapes, from the second half of the 1900s onward, the unchangeable traditional aesthetics is being displaced, an aesthetics of universal values and univocal design, to which is tied an abstract urban planning based on collaboration between the arts and science, between technology and representation, and on multiform designs. The size of the expanding city emphasizes its deconstructive aspects in a dynamics of practices and a plasticity dictated by the speed of change. If we interpret the situation through the questioning gaze described above, we will find an art of the city that can exist alongside the arts of painting, sculpture, architecture, literature, dance, and theatre – an art charged, in this case, with a high degree of improvisation. Movement governs the rich play of synaesthesia in which the inhabitant or the visitor becomes the protagonist, in a sense, along with the forms of the city. This movement is not left to itself, but is subjected to the participatory gaze of the people. I am referring to the spontaneous movements of citizens who themselves become active architecture, as in New York's High Line Park (an aerial greenway).

Romano (1993, 135) has written that the order of the city is not a crystalline, morphological order, such as that of Newton's, associated with the concept of land-use planning. Rather, it is compensative, and it consists of the rules of its own transformation, which is to say, norms with unpredictable effects that produce a broken, rather than linear, pace of development, giving rise to instability and a quest for permanence. These norms are embedded in the quantity, form, and arrangement of the city's visible objects, and are crystallized in the course of the long life of the urban cosmos through the perpetuation of safeguarded inhabited land, in response to the demand for meaning on the part of its citizens. A city survives if its citizens can satisfy their need for meaning and if they can build their houses with a "minimum" of aesthetic freedom, to produce perpetually new and sufficient collective ties in which the feeling of belonging to a *civitas* can materialize. Otherwise, they remain prisoners in metropolitan ghettos or exiles in the nondescript bedroom communities on the outskirts of the city. We can think of the chaotic growth of the city not only as disastrous disorder, but also as an opportunity to rethink urban society in terms of giving sense to the experience of daily life.

In addition, the current aesthetic stirs up thoughts of mobile holograms, and is fascinated by a lab-created copy, that is, the clone. It is engaged in a *poiesis* or creativity lacking feeling or passion, which results in the flood of postmodern excesses, the feverish mixing of technology and a lush green economy. This seems to be a genius for cloning and holograms, but it is up to us to produce different creative practices. We have as examples Friedensreich Hundertwasser's apartment block, Patrick Blanc's green walls, Emilio Ambasz's green architecture, Edouard François's façades, and the bands of vegetation in the architecture of Terunobu Fujimori and, to an extent, Rem Koolhaas.

With their enigmatic and hidden beauty, the solid forms of the city, whether fantastic or illusionistic, offer themselves to the observer, who is reminded of a film or literary description. In the megacities of the world, whose forms create evocative and stimulating images, we feel like protagonists on the natural stage of the world. My call for a new *flânerie* is a response to the various images offered up by the media and their stimulating communication strategy, which is based in being persuasive, as happens often with architectural structures on one hand, and fascination, as in the non-material dimension of the written word, on the other.

In the context of an analysis of money, Simmel (1987, 41), in the early part of the 1900s, raised the question of the problem of technology and described the sense of disquiet, located beneath the threshold of consciousness, of those who sense the loss of something definitive and are seeking out new stimuli, emotions, activities, and variety in a flow of tastes and convictions. In his *The Metropolis and Mental Life* (1995), Simmel speaks of the "intensification of the nervous life" in the megacities, which results in an obtuseness in the face of difference, wherein meaning is erased by the money economy in an unending creation of new needs. Megacities are the site of the money civilization, which transcends and crushes all personal elements. Simmel's comment on the nature of the city – a question he poses in the opening chapter of *Metropolis* – remains illuminating today:

The most significant aspect of the metropolis lies in this functional magnitude beyond its actual physical boundaries and this effectiveness reacts upon the latter and gives to it life, weight, importance and responsibility. A person does not end with the limits of his physical body or with the area to which his or her physical activity is immediately confined but embraces, rather, the totality of meaningful effects that emanate from him or her temporally and spatially. In the same way the city exists only in the totality of the effects which transcend their immediate sphere. This

really is the actual space in which their existence is expressed. (Ibid., 17)

In a short piece on the topic of bridges and doors, Simmel
(1970) also explains that everything in nature has value, whether
in connection with other things or in isolation. The appearance
of things has this dual meaning for us. Only humankind has the
ability to link things together or to disassemble them in this
particular way. A thing exists in relation to another, and all the
individual things taken together constitute a cosmos. Streets,
bridges, and doors are the points of communication, a physical
and symbolic linkage unmediated by abstract reflection. They
are an appearance that subsumes the meaning of practical
intent. The bridge accentuates separation and eliminates the
distance between two supporting points by making it visible.
The door demonstrates how separating and joining are two
aspects of the same action. Human beings, who were the first
to erect a door and to build a road, affirmed this specifically
human power in the face of nature, cutting a particular segment
from the infinite expanse of space and shaping it in accordance
with a specific sense or meaning. In opening onto limitless
space and closing to limited space, both of which are aspects we
find in people and in nature, doors are an integral part of
human activity. Doors, roads, bridges, and houses constitute the
creative act that is the basis of the city, an intersection of relationships and objects, a place to inhabit and pass through, a
dynamic whole of visible forms. Infinity and finitude coexist as
an active hope. In Simmel's words:

Man is a limited being that has no limits. His being-at-home
through the door means that he has detached a fragment
from the uninterrupted unity of natural being. But, just as
the informal limit becomes a Form, the limits of the latter
acquires its meaning and value only in that which the
movement of the door makes possible; that is, in the possibility of throwing himself into each moment, outside of this
limit and into freedom. (Ibid., 8)

The human being is likewise the bordering creature who has no border. The closing off of his or her domestic being, as if by a door, means, to be sure, that they have separated a piece from the uninterrupted unity of natural being. But just as the formless limitation takes on a shape, its limited nature finds significance and dignity only in that which the manoeuvrability of the door illustrates: the possibility at any moment of stepping out of limitation into freedom (Frisby and Featherstone 1997, 174).

BEYOND THE SYMBOL: DESOLATION AND HELL

I have discussed the city, the history of the city, celestial cities like Jerusalem and Angkor Wat, real cities, and imagined cities. But there are also apocalyptic cities, such as the hell of the poor described in the film *The Millionaire*, and cities of desolation, such as the tent cities of refugees and those fleeing war zones. In the case of the latter, some might say that we are not dealing with cities, but I would like to stress that thousands of people brought together in one place with a minimum degree of cohabitation can constitute a dignified, though wounded, community. A minimal amount of planning designed to establish social relations is the basic step in the creation of a city as a place in which to live. These are spaces where many people wait and hope to one day be able to return to their homeland and go back to their homes. If we think of the most degraded areas of the globe, the *favelas* (slums) of South America, the slums of India, and the hardships faced by those who live there, we have an image of great suffering, which cannot but move human civilization. We can go anywhere on earth and see tragic conditions, such as those in Wim Wenders's documentary *Salt of the Earth*, which portrays the photographs of Sebastião Salgado. In addition to cities of squalor, we also find cities of intolerance, divided by walls, both visible and invisible, and cities mutilated by fratricidal conflict, such as Jerusalem, Beirut, Belfast, and Nicosia.

We are strongly affected by the sight of cities turned into war zones with vast areas of architectural skeletons and piles of rubble. We surely remember the ruins of Dresden and a levelled Berlin at the end of the Second World War, and more recently, Kabul. The symbol of enormous tragedy, however, is Hiroshima, which was completely destroyed by the atomic bomb. These are cities stripped of their sense of belonging and identity, wretched reminders of devastation and death. Such images illustrate the unending grief of human history, the shocking face of horror, and the end of all spiritual or symbolic meaning. Once they have arisen from the ashes, cities dedicate memorials to their wounds: urban memorials like the one in New York at the World Trade Center, erected after the attack on the Twin Towers in 2001, and trans-urban memorials for entire populations, like the Holocaust Memorial or the Jewish Museum in Berlin. The first is the work of Davis Brody Bond, head of a team of architects and designers; the second is the work of Peter Eisenman, and the third of Daniel Libeskind.

It sometimes happens that, instead of remembering, people want to sever their ties with the past. To forget the atrocities by decree is an ancient propensity. Thrasybulus was perhaps the first to do so in 403 BCE, using a strategy designed to create a peaceful society following the civil war. The democratic party, which was victorious in that year against the bloodthirsty oligarchy of the Thirty Tyrants, swore to "reconcile the atrocities" by granting amnesty to all who had been a part of the old regime. Among those who have written about this are Nicole Loraux, who has analyzed the politics of ancient Athens with regard to stagnation, internecine war, and the relationship between remembrance and erasure of the past; and Marco Filoni, who examines the phenomenon of fear in the city as he rethinks the relationship between order and place, and between social norms and inhabited space. Indeed, the fundamental problem of dwelling is growing in the global age. There is a profound connection between space and land, which increasingly requires us to be custodians of the land by cultivating it or otherwise intervening in it, to take care of that which has always been all around us. But what is the sense of taking care if we ignore a very important, albeit dangerous, human emotion such as fear? Are we dealing with a fusion of humanity and history, or a flight from memory? Can civilization progress by giving itself over to fear, or, rather, to preservation and memory? What role does cultural transformation play in today's society in the face of terror, which threatens to destroy not just a social group or population, but its identity as well? These are crucial questions to which there are a number of answers. In places where conflict and peace among peoples, nations, and communities have alternated over a long period of time, memory and erasure of the past have been the two main instruments used by civilization to stem the resurgence of hatred and the thirst for vengeance. Remembering and forgetting seem to be undisputed remedies for the ills of the world. They seem to be entirely laic practices but are, in fact, inspired by the spirituality of the noblest religious traditions.

We carry with us catastrophic images when it comes to the current climate of tension in the world, which generates great fear in the megacities. The anguish that comes from the sense of danger is everywhere and triggers the imagination to conjure up the spectre of a collective panic, which, paradoxically, becomes an agent of social cohesion; what destroys also unites. Fear is a contagion created by the shock of a lack of protection; in that moment, laws and the natural order seem to have disappeared. Who can say whether it is better to respond to this obsession with acts of courage or irony, with political and military interventions, or the artifice of art? Fortunately, acts of courage are not only military; the construction of memory involves monuments and museums, as noted above. We cannot evoke the memory of an event by preserving entire sections of a city destroyed by war, cordoning them off, and leaving them the way they are. Rebuilding such areas is a collective psychological imperative. We cannot, therefore, imagine entire cities left in ruin, prey to the passage of time, as though they were enormous temples dedicated to remembrance. In some cases, we may wish to preserve only some eloquent ruins, and this suffices, as in

Berlin, or Kobe where, following an earthquake, a piece of road in the port area was left cracked and raised, alongside street-lights twisted by the seismic force. The moment of the disaster is frozen in time, consisting of objects that survived and a tangible memory.

Among all the cities of the world and in human history, Hiroshima stands today as an unsurpassed image of immense devastation, preserved in two museums and a great square of peace. The Hall of Remembrance, built in 2002 and designed by Kenzō Tange, revives the ancient concept of the mausoleum. The memorial consists of an underground circular structure with twelve columns supporting the ceiling, with a basin in the centre. Visitors access this site through a long, curved hallway, like a pilgrimage route. On the walls all around is installed a panorama of the city as it was after the explosion of the atomic bomb, viewed from the hypocentre, using 140,000 tiles, which is the estimated number of victims. Both a memorial and a temple of peace, as well as a place of silence and meditation, the monument joins together in a universal concept from antiquity, the West and the East. In one inspired image, it symbolically embraces all human beings on the planet. It is a circle of echoes, the haunting echoes of human history, and it has the spiritual aura of a *tholos* (beehive tomb), or a hypogeum that tells the story of a tragic event turned into myth. All humankind is represented in the nightmare of death and guilt. In this city is also another museum of remembrance, the Hiroshima Peace Memorial Museum, which was built between 1950 and 1955, and was also designed by Kenzō Tange. Here we see how the ancient can be the foundation for the modern; here, for instance, the project reflects the typical local architecture. The Japanese architect seems to have been inspired by the Itsukushima Shrine, located about thirty kilometres away, a space that is divided by covered walkways, like bridges to the sea and the sky. Rhythmically broken up by the piers that support the roof, the walkways also allow visitors to view the territory around the temple: nature extending in the form of landscapes and gardens of various sizes. Here the small and the infinitely large are interchangeable with respect to the eye and the mind. Like the walkway, the bridge spontaneously establishes a relationship that invites us to imagine places of remembrance and celestial places, sacred sites, and sites of change. In this temple, the walkways embrace the *torii* or "floating" gate in the middle of the inland sea. The essential design of the Hiroshima Peace Memorial Museum reflects this place and arrays the architectural elements horizontally. With its moral and spiritual meaning, the museum houses our memory as the point where an awe-inspiring emptiness of the cosmos converges with the signs of human activity. The walkway symbolizes a passage through sites of meditation and ritual, and at the same time creates avenues of serenity and splendour in the midst of unspeakable disaster.

Let us consider an example of a recent postwar city, to consider what happened and reflect on possible projects for a better future. I am referring to Beirut, where the reconstruction frenzy has not been taking into account the past, the superimposition of styles and forms, or the features of the city's architectural language prior to the disaster. Though suffering deep wounds from the bombardment – and Gabriele Basilico's photo "Beirut 1991-Rue Gourand" still fresh in our minds – the city has chosen to forget and to change its appearance in any way possible. The important thing is erasing the image of the past; people want to forget. The erasure of memory, however, is achieved, above all, through banal reconstruction and uncontrolled overbuilding. The city has rejected its architectural legacy as it rebuilds and turns to senseless construction. Having erased the past, the "new" marches on and seems directed at removing all obstacles to incomprehension, when in reality that incomprehension lurks and is ready to reassert itself. The civil war altered the internal equilibrium and relationships throughout the region. There were also countless exiles. Where is the old Beirut? What we can understand of the past appears only in Fouad Debbas's collection of photographs and postcards, which portray Beirut as it was before the war years. Today the city is characterized by a porous topography, as Lorenza Pignatti explains. The city has a strong attraction: alongside the Beirut torn by violence is a Beirut that is the Switzerland of the Middle East (though perhaps it no longer exists), which is to say an "Arabicized" and westernized Mediterranean metropolis.

In the course of fifteen years of war, 3,641 car bombs have been set off – a form of protest that Mike Davis has defined as the atomic bomb of the poor, killing 4,386 people. Always an exemplar of the cultural situation of the Middle East, owing to the particular composition of its society, comprising populations from eighteen different religions and a comparable number of ethnicities, Beirut is a phoenix that always rises from its ashes. Strategically important from both an economic and a political standpoint, the city has undergone a massive cycle of building in the last few decades, an intricate process in which complex economic and political factors are in play. Against a backdrop of bloody conflicts, a web of terrible contradictions has been woven, culminating in a full-scale reconstruction program. Rafic Hariri, prime minister from 1992 to 1998, re-elected in 2001, and assassinated in 2005, was one of the founders of Solidere (Société libanaise pour le développement et la reconstruction de Beyrouth) (The Lebanese Company for the Development and Reconstruction of Beirut Central District). Solidere was established in 1991 with the aim of rebuilding the central district of Beirut, which was repeatedly bombed during the civil war (1975 to 1990). Solidere erased the past and planned a city with new forms. To cite one example, for the Beirut Souks project, a large retail centre with more than 200 shops, what remained of the traditional *souks* (markets) was demolished. Although a few historic and religious buildings have been restored, as Pignatti informs us, Beirut remains a space of transformation, rather than a space of remembrance. We can think of it as a text or a palimpsest of histories and stories that reveals the traces of history even when it tries to erase them. Today the urban space is the sum of neighbourhoods that are like large boxes where the inhabitants are becoming strangers to one another. An extremely fragmented place, and one currently without a government, it seems to celebrate incomprehension and abuse of power.

Perhaps no city, particularly in the 1980s, has been the site of so many ideologies that are in competition with one another, with dozens of armed groups involved. In addition, there is no single reading of Lebanese culture, no history book officially recognized by the various religious groups – just as the Beirut National Museum displays works and artifacts from the prehistoric to the Medieval Mameluke period, but nothing from later epochs. In Lebanon, history is a political subject that is reflected in the country's life, culture, habits, art, and public spaces. Various artistic and urban development projects completed in recent years have probed not just the landscape but the difficulty of using space in a way that benefits citizens. During the civil war, the Green Line divided the city into East Beirut (predominantly Christian) and West Beirut (predominantly Muslim), thus splitting the centre into two zones via a clean demarcation line that bisected the east–west axis – a division still visible in the abandoned buildings along Rue de Damas. It has brought about the sectoring of the city and the destruction of public spaces, including the urban centre, in terms of mobility. Divided into factions, the citizens still seem unable to agree on a unified vision of their country, nor a collective identification.

These days, it is not pleasant to wander through the streets of Beirut the way one could in Victorian London, Baron Haussmann's Paris, or Franz Joseph's Vienna. These are definitely not places for quiet, enjoyable *flânerie*. In Beirut, streets have different names depending on the direction from which people enter them; the building numbers are sometimes missing, and there are no maps for some areas of the city, as indicated by the rePLACE BEIRUT project. Taxis move about the city without the aid of GPS, and only the downtown tourist area has recently been digitally mapped. Obsolete city maps and the difficulty of driving cars have become major problems that prompted rePLACE BEIRUT participants to create their own archive of places and paths in the urban space by which to know and narrate the city. In order to move about, it is necessary to identify the neighbourhoods and then the commercial activities (stores, restaurants, etc.) found in the vicinity. The taxi services, which replaced the public transit network (destroyed during the war and not rebuilt after 1990), were the topic of a workshop organized three years ago by the Dutch artist Bik Van der Pol. Geographers, urban planners, and topographers, along with artists, designers, non-governmental agencies, and journalists, have been attempting to circulate freely and to map the city. This is perhaps an indication of a rediscovered peace. In the past, one could travel from Beirut to Syria or Turkey by bus or train. Today, some parks and cemeteries are still closed. In order to understand Beirut, we could perhaps use new interpretive aids, such as Stefano Boeri's *atlanti eclettici* (eclectic atlases) from the late 1990s, in which he attempted in a new interdisciplinary way to examine the relationship between things and space, and between words and the things they indicate, as well as the associations the words produce. In this way, we can access a variety of materials, such as photographic documents, literary descriptions, or qualitative studies on the different cartographic practices, thereby avoiding a univocal and totalizing vision of the data. The objective is to invent what Pignatti calls a "collaborative cartography," starting with a census of empty space – and in Beirut there are so many, since the city has a porous topography that no official or method of scientific mapping has yet identified. Starting with empty spaces means that citizen participation can be reawakened and the soul of the city restored.

Alongside the possibilities offered by empty spaces, the response to the dissolution of a sense of place can involve the deconstruction of stereotypes – such as Beirut destroyed by war – and, in the case of Beirut, its reconstruction on the basis of historical documents and personal accounts. It seems that, in this way, the citizens of different communities can recognize themselves in an essential urban fabric and thereby rediscover, even if only provisionally, the symbolic value of places that epitomize collective memory. These include Martyrs' Square, built in 1916 to commemorate the revolution against the Ottoman empire; the monument erected in Sassine Square on the spot where President Bachir Gemayel was assassinated; the monuments dedicated to writer and journalist Samir Kassir and Gebran

Tueni, director of the daily newspaper *AnNahar*; and perhaps even the Holiday Inn and Murr Tower.

Following the assassination of Prime Minister Rafic Hariri, security measures increased exponentially and became elements of urban governance. The mission to protect members of various political institutions and religions, combined with a determination to limit the clash of different religious groups, has resulted in a redefining and narrowing of public space. Temporary checkpoints, blocked roads, inaccessible parking lots, surveillance cameras, and the presence of public and private armed forces everywhere are the most visible signs of this. There are increased searches in the commercial centres, banks, and shopping malls, while the areas occupied by the United Nations, police stations, and major political parties have been transformed into bunkers. What we can conclude from such a description of the situation, I cannot say, but we should never give up hope for a better world.

The preceding account reminds us of a video game that is psychologically rather harmful. We cannot believe it. We think we are watching a film, and yet it is reality, and the truth lies in the extremely grave reports we see. Are we in Minas Tirith, enchanted by the pen of Tolkien, author of *Lord of the Rings*, or in the destroyed and abandoned megacities amid the galaxies of *Star Trek: Enterprise*? Where does our imagination go when, perhaps in search of a refuge, it turns to virtual worlds, such as those in fantasy or science fiction novels, or in the deliriums of the digital world (on computers, iPhones, etc.)? Through a sort of double vision, human actions create moving images, but images that do not correspond to those in the real world. So, what is happening? Is the city still a habitable place or merely an illusory place? We find ourselves at the limit of what is possible. Imagination can help us to meditate on the flow of time and changing events and places, as long as we are aware of the difference between the real and the imaginary, as well as the distance separating them.

I have been arguing that in the case of Beirut, the symbolic structure is in crisis because the city as a system no longer corresponds to the perception and actions of its citizens. The sense of a shared social sphere and of civil understanding has disappeared. However, let me clarify the matter from an aesthetic point of view, which is to say, from the point of view of architecture and urban design. These are operational variables that depend on ethical and political processes, which have the power either to sabotage or to sustain their meaning, depending on the social weight given to the projects. In the new buildings erected after the civil war, we see, in essence, a creative void in search of a symbolic point of convergence: a time of waiting for objects to configure themselves in such a way as to create a collective identity. In Beirut, architecture is in chaotic transition. The symbolic structure of the city that people want to encounter, the city as a system of forms, is lost in the confusion.

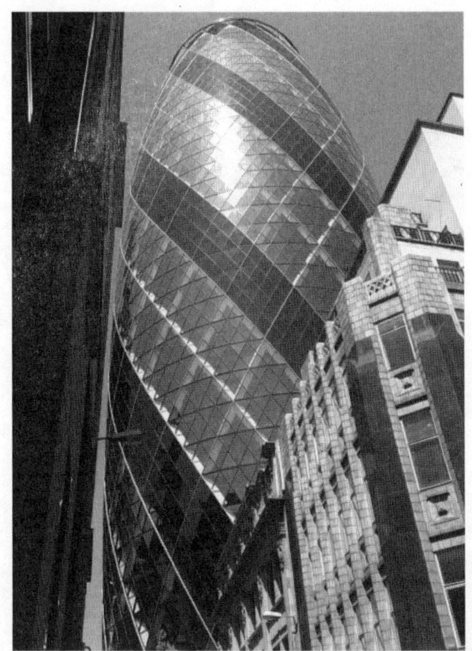

7a London, The Gherkin (architects Norman Foster and Ken Schuttlesworth, 2004)

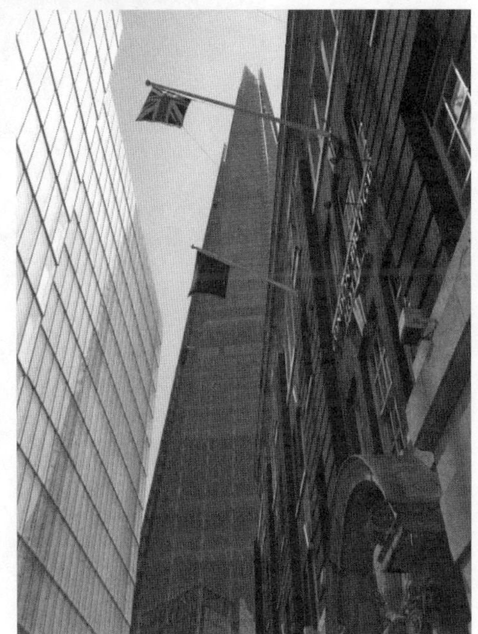

7b London, The Shard (architect Renzo Piano, 2012)

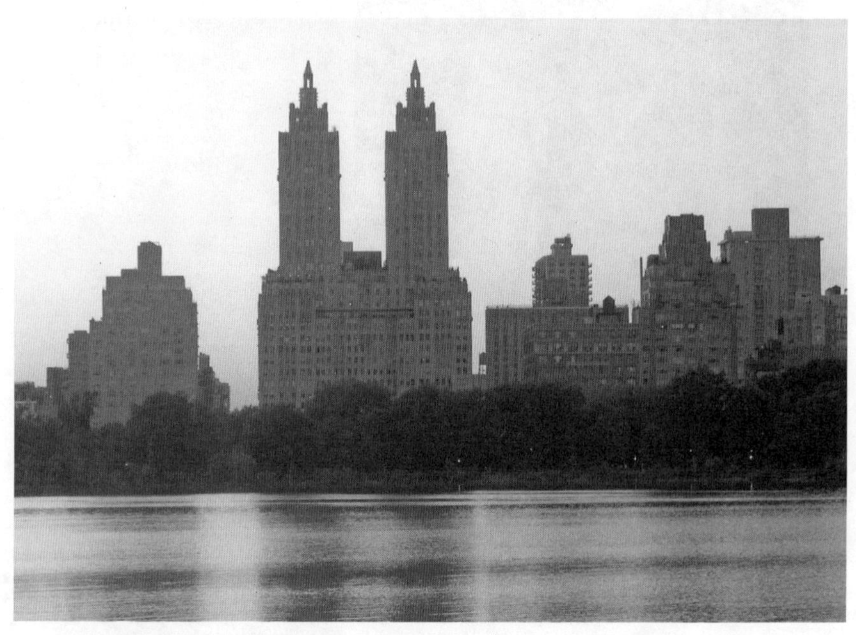

8a New York, Manhattan, Central Park

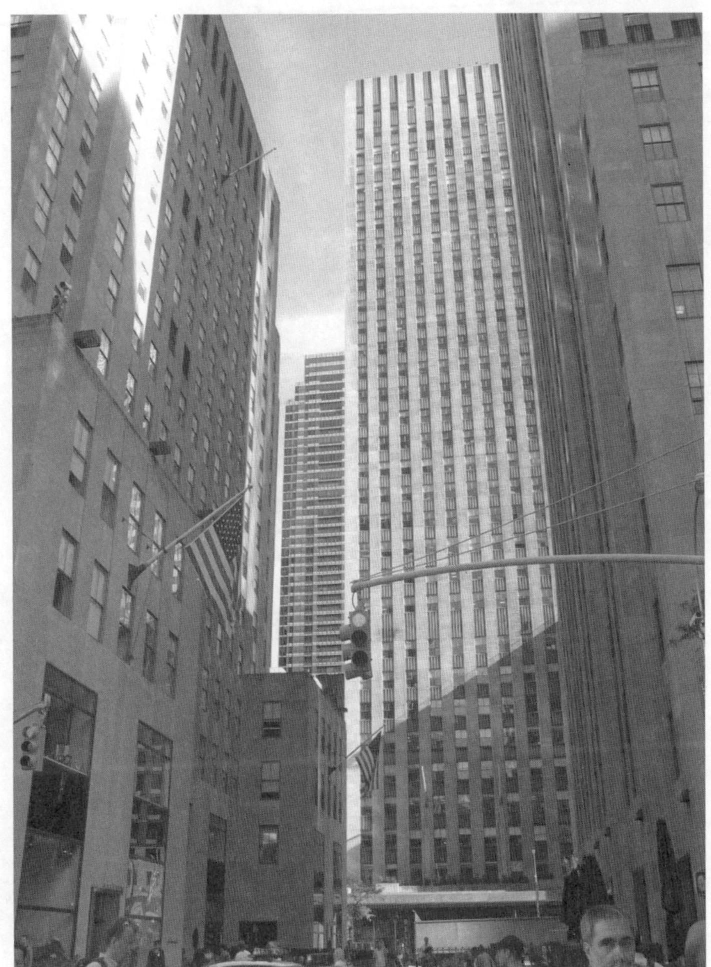

8b New York, Manhattan, skyscraper

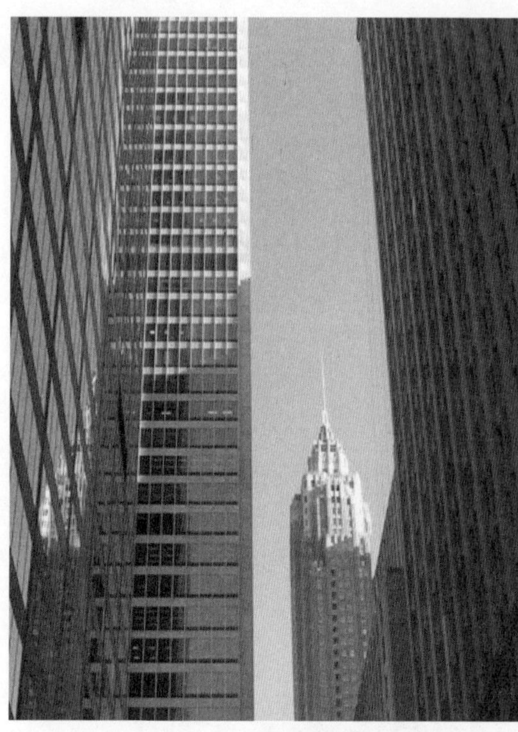

8c New York,
Manhattan,
skyscraper

8d New York,
Rockefeller Center,
Winged Mercury

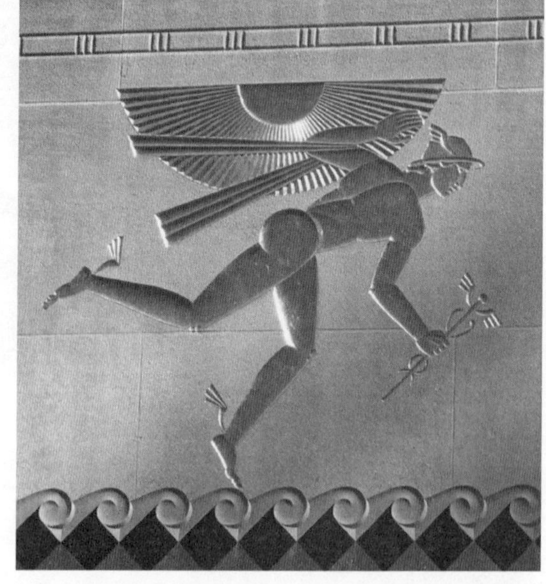

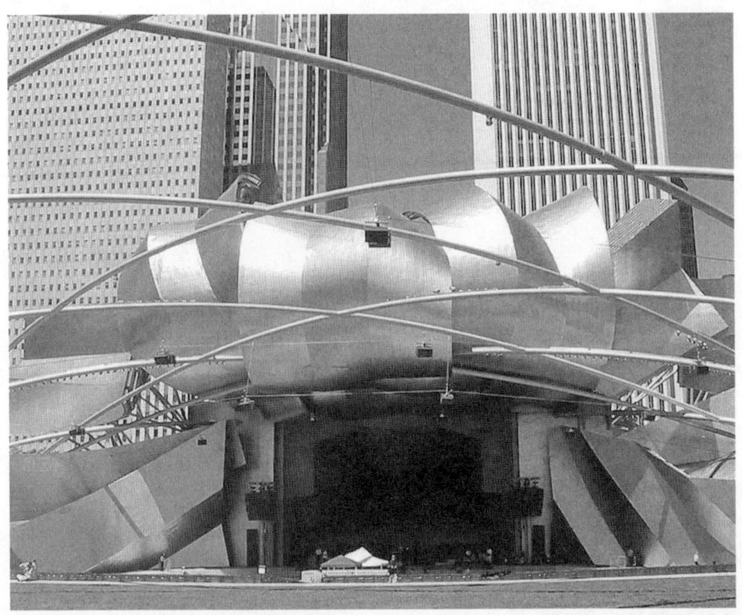

9a Chicago, Millennium Park, Jay Pritzker Pavillion (architect Frank Gehry, 2004)

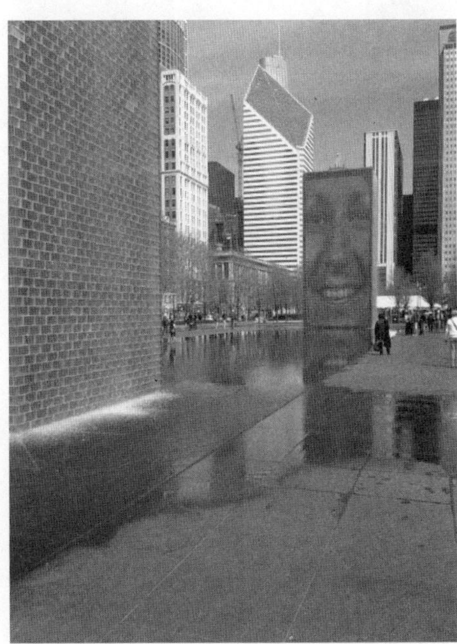

9b Chicago, Millennium Park, Crow Fountain (designed by Jaume Plensa, 2004)

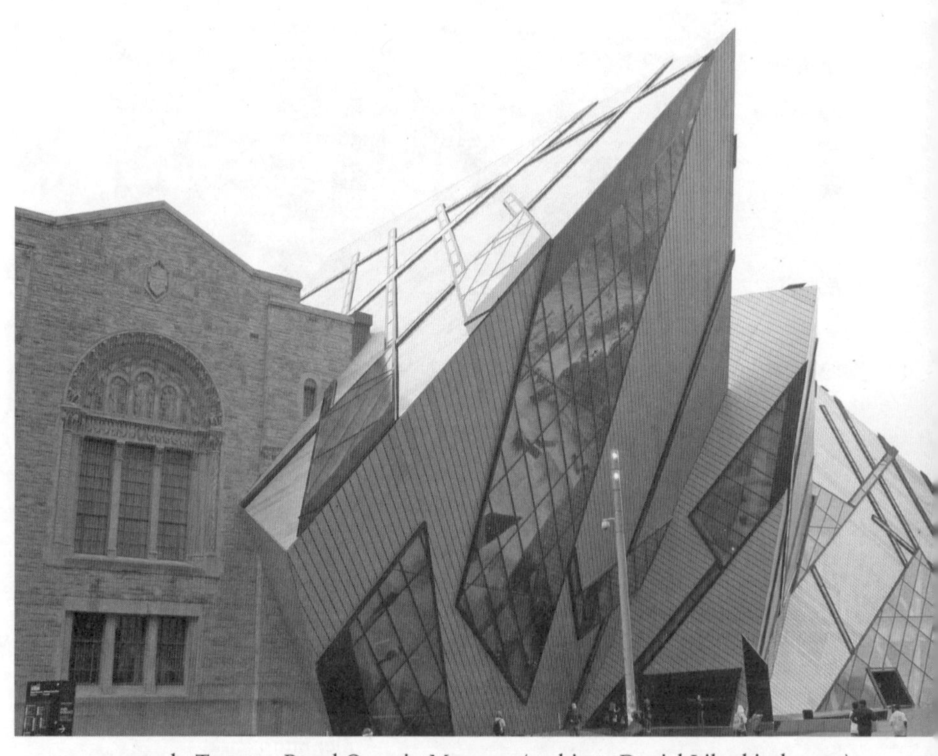

10a, 10b Toronto, Royal Ontario Museum (architect Daniel Libeskind, 2010)

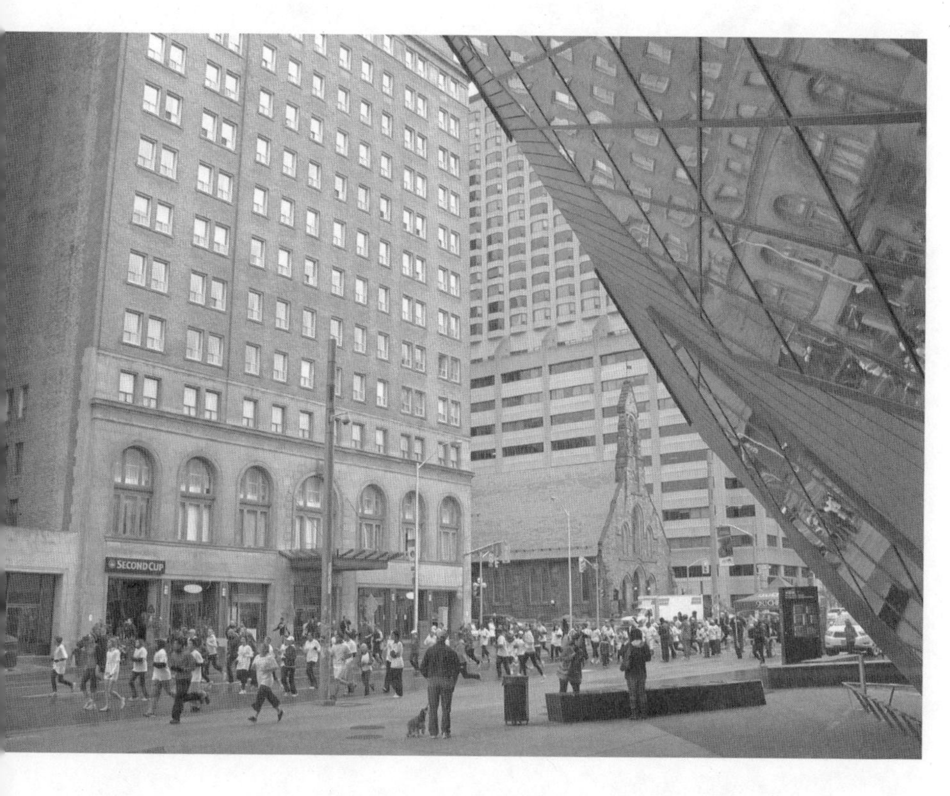

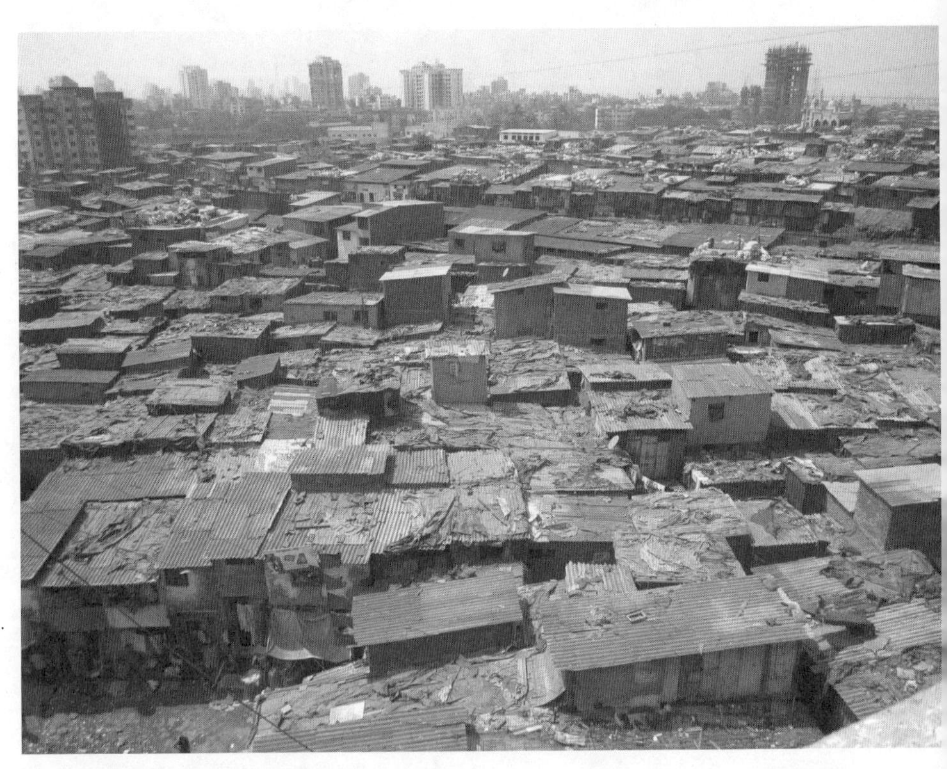

11 Slum in Mumbai

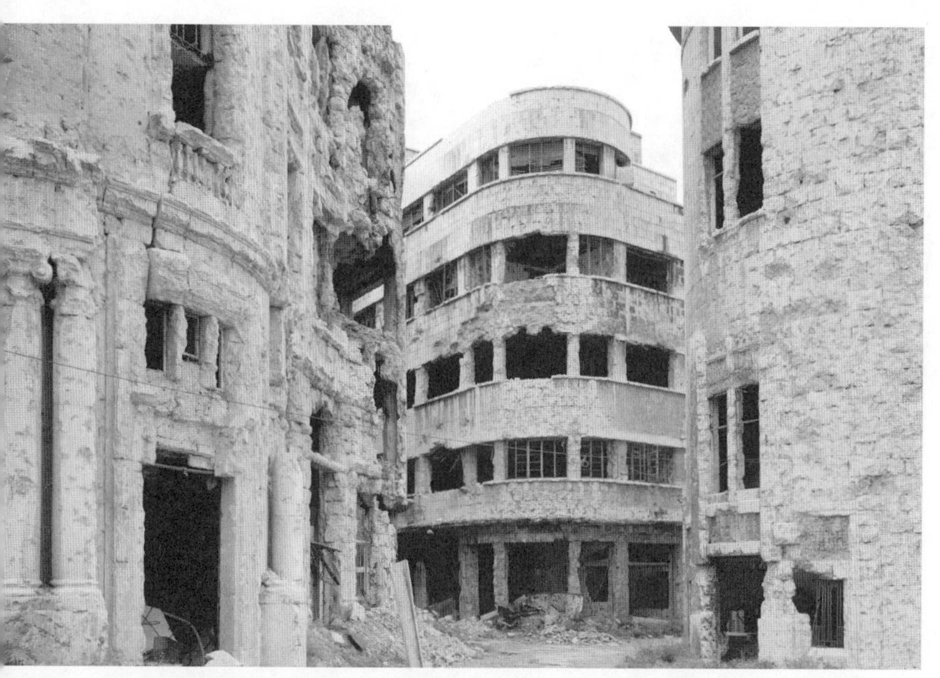

12 Beirut (Photo by Gabriele Basilico, 1991)

2

What Is the City?

A discussion of the idea of the city brings to mind a useful concept from Plato. Just as the *aréte* (excellence) of a certain man-made object is the fruit of the technical skill that instilled in that object the *eidos* (the form perceived by the intellect) of the model that guided its operations, so the *aréte* of politics is the fruit of the technical skill that instilled in its object the *eidos* of justice. The result is the institution of order in objects and human actions. The two elements of this reflection, the object and politics, remind us of the correlation between *urbs* and *civitas*, discussed earlier – that is, the stones and the institutions of the city. In the previous chapter, I described the form of the city, which is to say, the way it acquires form in history. I have explored *how* the city is. Now we need to understand *what* it is. What is the idea of the city?

Some, like Rosario Assunto, contend that prior to industrialization, the city was the space of representation, whereas after industrialization and in the age of globalization, it is merely the space of "the useful." The idea of the city, therefore, is formed and then transformed into representation: a universe of meaning that humankind has been able to construct over time. Fustel de Coulanges (1830–1889) used the term "holy city" to describe Athens, the Greek city about which Thucydides and

Aristotle also wrote, where there is a relationship between the *polis* (city) and the *polites* (citizens) because power resides with the people in the Athenian democracy. All the citizens are equal before the law, and in the army (in Athens the citizens are also soldiers), responsibilities, merit, and ability erase all differences between the rich and the poor. *Philotimia* (love of honour) is the virtue of the citizens, and in a democratic *polis* it is expected that freedom, equality, friendship, and unity should prevail. For Aristotle (*Politics, Nicomachean Ethics*), the city naturally invites people to form a community for the common good. The *polis* is considered to be a natural community on the road to perfection. In its infinity, time is rendered symbolically as a planimetric image, that is, a square for the Romans, in accordance with an archetype based on cosmological principles. Throughout the Christian era, the geometric centre contained a symbolic depiction of the *Cosmocrator* ("Ruler of the World"), sometimes flanked by the progenitors of the human race. Both Constantine's imperial city, depicted in the basilica of Santa Pudenziana in Rome, and the late-Gothic city we admire in Jan van Eyck's *Adoration of the Mystic Lamb* are mimetic, in the Platonic sense, that is to say, they imitate the heavenly Jerusalem. The city is portrayed as an atemporal, sacred place and the object of endless contemplation. In the 1400s, Platonic *logos* reappears as the spatial representation of forms in the "Ideal City" fresco in Urbino, mentioned in the previous chapter. This is a story of beauty that assumes different forms: harmony in Leon Battista Alberti, grace in Marsilio Ficino, poetry in Palladio, whose project is that of harmonizing antiquity and nature, and finally the baroque machine with its celebration of architecture that imitates nature. Assunto makes the point that everyone enjoyed the ancient city, not just the rich, whereas today the order has been reversed, in that the useful precedes representation. Today, most people are excluded from this process, and Bacon's "philosophy of the useful" degenerates with the passage of time into the powerful image of Prometheus the builder, which drives the joy of contemplation from the mind. It is argued by some that the mass production of goods, urban expansion as far as the eye can see, the destruction of what is beautiful and nature, the triumph of the machine, the deterioration of historic centres, and the overemphasis on functionality have led to the obliteration of the dignity of urban life. There is the sense, however, that such an interpretation idealizes the past and tradition.

Massimo Cacciari's (2004, 7–13) interpretation of the culture of the ancient world is perhaps more problematic and less directly oppositional, given that for him the city does not exist; rather there are different and distinct forms of urban life. He identifies the Greek *polis* as the site where the *ethos* of a given people, as defined by their traditions and customs, resides. He maintains that such ontological and genealogical specificity is not contained in the Latin word *civitas* (citizenship), which is essentially the *cives* (citizens) coming together to give themselves the same laws. The Romans were governed by the same law, irrespective of ethnicity and religion. The Greeks considered the city to be a unity of the same kind of people. The *polis* referred to an organic whole that preceded the citizen, and for this reason each *polis* was isolated from the others, in spite of the festivals and Olympics, as were the federations, which did not last long. In the *polis*, those who were free but did not belong to a *genos* (race) were considered *metics* (foreign residents) or guests. In the Roman Empire, citizenship among freedmen was not based on ethno-religious criteria but on a strategic *concordia* (agreement) between the parties established by law. In this regard, the constitution of Caracalla in the first decades of the third century is interesting in that it applied to all freedmen throughout the Empire. In this respect, the origins of Rome, too, are particularly illuminating in that different peoples were involved in the founding of the city. The Trojans were victorious by divine will, but were destined to be absorbed into the language and names of the Latin tribes.

The modern European perspective grew out of the Roman practice and is centred on a precise idea, as Cacciari explains (ibid., 23): as in the writings of Augustine, the city of man and the city of God will continue to be based not on ethnic criteria, but over the course of time will feel the pain of "nostalgia for the *polis*." In another twofold concept, the city is, on the one hand, the place where we find ourselves in a type of womb, a feminine and maternal house (as we see in some small Sahrawi or Tuareg cities of North Africa). On the other hand, the city is a function of or an instrument for commercial transactions. The city is both *otium* (leisure) and a network of *negotia* (business transactions). From the 1400s to the 1900s, the idea of the city as the seat of commerce and business prevailed. In recent decades, since the traditional *forma urbis* (model of the city) has disappeared, the need to amalgamate *otium* and *negotium* in a renewed art of the city has taken hold. The need is for the restoration of order to both things and habits, as well as for an enlightened politics that can balance destructive and innovative practices. This may be a contradictory expectation, but it is a useful one. The modern and the postmodern city has lost the aura of place, its symbolic meaning, and its collective spirit tied to actual life, and what is emerging is an undifferentiated mass, the outflow of an economy of consumption.

What is architecture in the postmodern era, or better yet, what is the relationship between thought and architecture now that the ideal city of the Renaissance, the hyperbolic baroque city, the rationalization of urban space in the 1800s, the concept of the *cité mondiale* (world city), the provisions of the Athens Charter, and the modernist project of Le Corbusier have been eclipsed? Jacques Derrida (2008) has called attention to the deconstructive aspect of thought with his notion of text and space, pointing out that in the spatial arts, thought is or may already be incorporated in the artwork. The question of architecture is inseparable from that of the city. Any discussion of man-made goods must also involve the urban and natural context in which they are introduced.

Faced with the emptiness of the present, I will invoke a useful piece of advice from the past. In the works of Lewis Mumford, I have found a valid point of view from which to reorient my current observations, and to identify three primary functions of the city, as it pertains to education: 1) the city as education, whose purpose is to recover an historical identity entwined with personal biography; 2) the city that, in its context, promotes education through experiences and tests; and 3) the city that puts universal moral principles into practice, principles that are related in particular to the sharing of social responsibilities (people as full-fledged citizens). These functions relate to the project of living in common. The cities scattered throughout the world seem familiar, attractive, beautiful, or ugly, depending on how someone feels, lives, and moves about. The movement of the inhabitant, like the wanderings of the *flâneur*, gives value to places, making them meaningful. Empty city squares, abandoned houses, and streets in disrepair are not merely backdrops; rather, they are settings in which the citizen is a protagonist, both in historical cities and cities such as New York or Tokyo. A kind of "narrative art" is activated in the temporal and spatial coordinates of experience, thus helping reacquire a sense of identity, in that analogies, discoveries, realizations, and shared experience come into play on a mental and physical level. Windows and portals allow us to enter and exit courtyards, houses, and public spaces, like a character in a video by Bill Viola, an artist who effectively portrays this disquiet, and at the same time this attempt to attain personal and collective redemption in the universe of the multitudinous.

The city is being progressively extinguished by its ubiquity. It is always expanding, and everything in it is becoming increasingly similar as a result of globalization. Since it is everywhere, it no longer exists. Only the post-metropolitan territory-habitat is emerging, with no discernible correlation to functions, relations, works, quality of construction, and quality of life. We must, therefore, invent "structures" that will enable us to live better and to consolidate the place where both the individual and the collective reside within truly multifunctional buildings, so that space is not reduced or suffocated, and time is not burned away by the speed of consumption. For these reasons, we should seek to reinforce the sense of being rooted in a place – the seat of human emotions, and the foundation of urban life – since in the last few decades we have only encountered processes that promote the uprooting of that sense. In the face of disorientation and a deadening of consciousness in the postmodern megacity, we can turn to the distant, utopian thought of Frank Lloyd Wright, as interpreted by Siegfried Giedion (2008, 123–33). For Wright, asphalt must disappear, and we need to produce buildings in the urban setting that are designed in such a way as to not suffocate the terrain and the landscape. Their form, that is, the relationship among objects, will emerge from a spatial conceptualization that adheres to a principle of harmony, the pursuit of complementarity between form and function, emotional needs, and sociologically necessary structures and relationships. Even the most beautiful residential neighbourhood must have a heart, which is to say, it must be a place that connects the private and the public life. The city is the primary symbol of differentiated human cohabitation. Giedion writes:

> Its heart is an eminently human problem. The degree to
> which this heart is filled with warm life depends on
> humans. Architects and urban planners know that they are
> not capable of solving this problem on their own: they
> need the help of sociologists, doctors, and, in a sense, historians too. (Ibid., 138)

We need to believe that the citizen wants to participate in the life of the city and wants to play the part that he or she has the right to play. This will compensate for the unease caused by the architectural forms in neighbourhoods built in the last few decades. People react to the desolation and repetitiveness of the most banal building stereotypes.

In talking about a continuous loss of meaning with regard to the city, we can look to the words of the urban planner Kevin Lynch (*The Image of the City*, 1960). For him, the city is not merely an object of perception (and perhaps of enjoyment) for millions of profoundly different people in terms of character and social class, it is also the product of countless agents that have been constantly changing its structure for specific reasons. In general, the city can remain stable for a period of time, and in some of its aspects for a long period of time. Its growth and power appear to be only partly controlled. There is no final result, only an endless series of phases. This is what Lynch wrote in 1960, and we see for ourselves that it is true.

Turning to philosophy, which has anticipated many of the valid observations on the evolution of modern urbanism, when it comes to dealing with the crisis in modernity we can look to the works of Simmel, Weber, and Durkheim, who offer some of the most important interpretations of the twentieth century. Theorizing a universal interaction and interpenetration of all phenomena, forming a web of reciprocal effects, Simmel discusses the metropolis and the life of the mind in the early part of the last century, taking as his starting point the thoughts he expressed in his *Philosophy of Money* (1900). He analyzes the fundamental aspects of modernization as they relate to the scale and organization of labour, as well as the relationship between money and rationality. For him, the division of labour brings about the fragmentation of social life and encourages individualism and egoism. Since it is impersonal, money reduces all things to a quantitative factor and leads to the hypertrophy of objective culture and the atrophy of subjective culture. The modern city, in other words the metropolis, fosters alienation. Both the family and the neighbourhood lose their importance as they are replaced by a myriad of superficial contacts. The metropolitan individual leads a frantic life: images strike his or her nervous system, causing a reduced ability to react to stimuli (the blasé attitude); thus, the individual is forced to seek refuge in interstitial spaces, where he or she searches for an "elsewhere," a place where the environment does not condition him or her in a severe fashion.

We know that the city can be good for society, but we also know that it can be harmful. To state it another way, it can contain a treatable illness, as Joseph Rykwert has said (2002, 243–50). We may ask what sacredness of space means once it is identified with the urban environment, with respect to its bodies and rituals. As has been said, even the city is a symbolic system. We might recall in particular what Rykwert said in a lecture on Freud on this topic, which is that the monuments and works of art found in a city can be mnemic symbols. For example, Charing Cross (formerly Eleanor Cross) is a monument in London that commemorates the funeral procession of Queen Eleanor, held in the thirteenth century; a cross was erected at each station where the procession stopped overnight along the road to Westminster. Not far from London Bridge is another cross that was erected to remind people of the fire of 1666. Today, people pass quickly through these places, but a few individuals, labelled neurotic or hysterical by Freud, still have "emotional" ties to these images. It is important to stress that there exists an intimate familiarity with the mnemic quality of such monuments. It is a form of identification with the city on the part of visitors and citizens alike, an identification that is renewed through processions and festivals. This creates personal, long-lasting symbolic meanings with an emotional resonance that is more or less latent. The idea of the city, therefore, is also the city we feel and represent through secret correspondences with the real map of streets, squares, monuments, and events made concrete at a specific point in space (for instance, the place where Julius Caesar was assassinated). In short, we infer a cultural dependence from existing structures (in stone or wood) that are deposited by history, along with memories that can be intuited or reconstructed. Moving backwards in an anthropology of the urban forms found in the ancient world, perhaps we can say that the city is a form of collective writing, given the conceptualization of space that has been planned out and built upon and has evolved. We can also say that the rhythm of modular buildings was transmitted to the first instances of hieroglyphics and cuneiform writing. The urban complex, therefore, has deep roots.

Following these comments on Rykwert, I now turn to Cacciari's observation, but by instead posing it as a question: If the design is universal, why are all cities different? And if they are different, why is the form that guided city founders from the beginning so important? By superimposing various cities that have succeeded one another throughout history, cultural anthropologists can account for both the diversity and the recurring model. Conquerors destroy and rebuild, and each in their own way coalesces the energy, value, and violence in a monument or several monuments, the interpretation of which allows us to make sense of the city as the organization of forms into a complex and organic concept. Squares, rectangles, and circles are superimposed on one another in search of other resonances, rhythmic juxtapositions, or calculated arrhythmias, forming a string of symbolic and ritualistic processes in which belief blends with the imagination. As Rykwert states:

> It is difficult to think that the order and regularity of the universe can be reduced to the schema produced by the two axes that intersect on a plane: and yet, this is indeed what happened in antiquity. The ancient Romans knew that the *cardo* on which they walked ran parallel to the axis around which the sun rotated, and they knew to follow its course when it moved along the *decumanus*. On the basis of their civic institutions, they were able to decipher the meaning of the cosmos, and this made them feel intimately connected to it. (1976, 261)

We in the modern world have lost this way of explaining the workings of the universe. Humanity, however, continues to shape the environment, giving it form even in the face of regular revisions by physicists. Rather than look for that explanation on the surface, people, by continuing to produce sculptures of the topography, will search for it by examining and rethinking themselves in terms of the dignity and responsibility of the person.

To take a different view, in the 1960s, Michel Foucault (2008, 45) contrasted space and history, but also space and architecture, stressing the importance of space over time and privileging labyrinthine figures, such as the Moebius strip or Escher's drawings: interlocking spaces that evoke a new dimension. Foucault wanted to avoid spatial-temporal dichotomies, such as sayable/unsayable, real/imaginary, and interior/exterior. He underscored the instability of the disintegrative processes of knowledge and power, an important pair of terms that highlight the structure of systems, the decision making of urban planners, which results in the loss of the sense of being. In the second half of the last century, space was considered heterogeneous rather than homogeneous; it emerges from utopia, a space lacking real places, and appears in heterotopia, a space that is rich in reality: hospitals, hotels, vacation spots, nursing homes, brothels, jails, barracks, convents, and cemeteries. Foucault made the following interesting observation: "The ship is heterotopia par excellence. In civilizations without boats, dreams dry up, espionage takes the place of adventure, and police take the place of pirates" (1997, 9). On this premise, how can we know what the French philosopher's idea of the city is? We can derive the idea only from the object. The city is a spatial projection, a form of reterritorialization whose true meaning lies in technical planning. The original autocratic city was a military camp, a fortress enclosed by thick walls. In contrast to this is the city of the Middle Ages, with its movement of collective systems that contain value in use and exchange: the street, square, cathedral, mill, library, agricultural knowledge, and the marketplace. How does urbanization today relate to the production system, and the management of wood and electrical technologies? History, in point of fact, never repeats itself, unless we are talking about a possible large-scale application of traditional technologies for ecological purposes. With regard to the city as a whole, we must agree with Foucault that architecture pertains to practical rationality directed toward a predetermined end (ibid., 71–2). Like the practice of government and other social organizations, architecture is a *techne* (craft) capable of using elements from sciences such as physics or statistics. A history of architecture is truly valuable if it is part of a general history of *techne*, and less so as a discipline linked to the exact sciences. Foucault's idea of the city can be summarized with his following comment on architecture and politics:

> Government is also a function of technologies: the government of individuals, the government of souls, the government of the self by the self, the government of families, the government of children. I believe that, if the history of architecture were to be located in the context of the general history of *techne*, in the broadest sense of the term, we could have a more interesting guiding concept situated between the exact sciences and the inexact sciences. (Ibid., 72)

In this sense, a solution that would seem to suit our epoch emerged in the last decade (though Foucault could not know this): the "smart city," a network of models of participation with innovations from the technical and programmatic point of view (already present in the Common Ground exhibit at the Venice Architecture Biennale, directed by David Chipperfield), constituting a transition from the material to the non-material. This, however, appears to be more of a technological vision dominating urban life than a balance of forces in the organization of city life in terms of quality of living. Foucault had in mind the government of the soul in a positive sense, a government of behaviours, and forms of knowledge, as well as the inventive and normative capacity of the world, in a complex interaction between the community and power in the strict sense of the word.

How can we examine the postmodernity of the metropolises and megalopolises in the age of globalization in the presence of such historical cities as Jerusalem, Rome, and Istanbul, considering their respective strategies of civility and civilization, and the stratifications of different cultures, as their buildings attest? In Jerusalem, the ancient stones allow for the emergence of the walls of the kingdom of Ezekiel (seventh to sixth century BCE) in the place known as the Tower of David; in

Rome, they give prominence to the place of the myth of Romulus; in Istanbul, they are remnants of pre-Christian buildings as well as those that date back to the origins of civilization. How do we compare the cities of the last century with all their changes in terms of symbolism? Let us look at a few examples of more recent architectural works as we reflect on the value, or loss of value, in the global megacities and take into account the fact that cities have always been images of political and symbolic power, as well as concrete expressions of seduction and enchantment. Modernity has given us emblematic cases in the figurative and plastic arts, and today there are other art forms as well that show how the sense of anonymity – associated with multifunctional skyscrapers, large shopping centres, and airports defined by Augé as "non-places" – fades or disappears altogether. I have in mind the installations of sculptor Richard Wilson in Terminal 2 at Heathrow airport (Slipstream) and the sound installations of Brian Eno for the Los Angeles airport, as well as Norman Foster's architectural design of Beijing airport's international terminal, and Renzo Piano's designs at the Osaka airport. We can also consider Terminal 3 in Shenzhen, by Massimiliano Fuksas; the Musée des Confluences in Lyon, designed by the Coop Himmelb(l)au studio, resembling a crystal made of a thousand lights (or a spaceship, amplifying the effect of Frank Gehry's Guggenheim Museum Bilbao); the Shanghai Tower by the Gensler studio; the Olympic stadium in Beijing by Meuron; the enormous structure in the shape of a ribbon for the cctv (China Central TV) headquarters in Beijing, by Koolhaas/oma; and Jean Nouvel's National Art Museum of China building (under construction) in Beijing. The postmodernism of Beijing reflects the modernism of London or Paris between the 1800s and 1900s: gigantic undertakings designed to represent the power and the entertainment of the masses. I am also thinking of the planning of new market zones, such as the Markthal in Rotterdam, a re-imagining of the city of commerce, which has existed from the Middle Ages to the present. In the new millennium, the age of the cosmopolis, we are witnessing unforeseen ways of perceiving, thinking, and seeing the world. In this context we are seeing a rise in urban agriculture, with the planning of agro-ecological cities. However, going unnoticed are the vast expanses of common buildings, the undifferentiated construction that fails to take into account what lies beyond the visual field, and which disturbs us with the existential squalor it creates.

I can sum up my thoughts on the idea of the city in the following way. The city manifests its ambiguity as a place in which to reside through the exercise of power, the expression of the elite, and the emergence of cultural models that break with tradition through their homogeneous and heterogeneous structures. The tensions and conflicts that characterize it are, historically, both the product of a ruling group that splits internally, and the manifestation of different groups that fight among each other. The aristocracy, the middle class, and the leaders of totalitarian regimes are marked by divergent events and ideologies. The city, therefore, is the creation of the culture of the many by the elite few who represent them. In addition, architectural and urban structures are the domain of philosophy. As mentioned earlier, in the mid-1900s, Panofsky established a parallel between the dictates of Medieval scholasticism and the Gothic cathedrals, identified as intelligible systems characterized by formal hierarchies of their spaces and a harmonization of contrasts. This notion is complemented by a later, equally interesting, study by Marius Schneider on "Singing Stones," concerning the correlation between musical rhythm and the forms of Romanesque architecture. During the Renaissance, geometry, perspective, and mathematical order combined in the models generated by Italian architects: Leon Battista Alberti, Francesco di Giorgio Martini, and Filarete. This use of geometry, however, is not neutral because it is tied to the structure of the social hierarchy and the organization of the space that reflects that hierarchy. The ideal Renaissance city is a finite, delimited space. In the form of the city, there is a complete set of ideas destined to be developed by Descartes, Pascal, Newton, and Leibniz that would transform the Renaissance into the baroque: two forms of rationalization that should not be contemplated abstractly but rather in their practices and locations in a precise relationship between styles and countries, and styles and cities, in a discourse concerning both what has lived and what is living.

ON METAPHOR

Hans Blumenberg developed the theory of non-conceptuality, arguing that images and metaphors should not be considered to be provisional or incomplete phases in the formation of concepts, but rather a fundamental aspect of knowledge and philosophical discourse. Metaphor relates to the structure of our symbolic mind and the language of the subconscious, it turns toward the present but attends to what is absent, and says what it sees and what it does not see. A metaphor results when a word is used in a given context to say something other than what it means. This play between reality and fiction, whether intentional or unintentional, enables us to detach ourselves from the object by making present that which is absent, thereby providing a new idea; this implies a return to the object enriched by a different sensibility, one that is impalpable but necessary. Joining together as they do elements that are separate and different from one another, images are used to make sense of the unforeseeable. They are a way of distancing oneself, or pretending to distance oneself, in order to return to the object. The metaphor is an aesthetic medium. Thanks to this trope, fear is turned into pleasure, for example. This happens when we distance ourselves from what we perceive in order to go beyond the limits of the senses. In this way, people engage in a fantasy world of symbols, which they can use to stand for that which appears before their eyes. When we observe and contemplate a city, we read it as though it were a book: it seems to have a language with a rhetorical code, artificial and incomplete though it may be, linked to the variability of sentiments, but still always a language that pertains to things and relationships. This gives rise to what Blumenberg calls the unforeseeable.

In the mid-1970s, however, Paul Ricœur discussed the many modes of discourse and sought to describe the essence of metaphor, relating it to the languages of redefinition or transformation of reality. On the basis of these arguments, by which we abandon the habitual use of language, and the more recent remarks made by Blumenberg, cited above, we can reflect on the "rhetoric" of architecture and the form of the city, which are tangible, as well as on the intangible or symbolic expression of the places in a community. In this way, we capture new aspects of things that appear all around us and the change in the meanings of those things, in harmony with the intentions of the reader/observer or the architect/creator of the work.

How can we experience metaphor in a tangible way as we read the architectural and urban landscape? It might be useful to examine Gabriele D'Annunzio's Vittoriale degli Italiani (Shrine of Italian Victories), a monumental hillside estate in Gardone Riviera. Here, D'Annunzio created an ideal place of evocation and analogy by transforming the literary text into an architectural and panoramic one, thereby asserting the eloquence of nature, as though the plants and flowers, and the water and light, possessed a language.

Everything is natural because everything is profoundly cultural. This also applies to psychology, in terms of our mental habits. In certain conditions, observation and contemplation become a state of wonder before nature, which enables the observer to exchange the features of a landscape for those of their imagination and emotional state. We may replace a watery landscape with another watery landscape, a mountain panorama with another mountain panorama, see a Greek vista in a vista found in the region of Puglia, or feel that we are in Mongolia when we are, instead, in the Castelluccio valley, or we may exchange the forms and colours of a castle in the Tyrol for those of a Tibetan village, and so forth. This kind of experience is not so recent; rather, it has been a part of our ability to see and to express admiration for many centuries. We need only consider Hadrian's Villa and the cult of commemorating myths, which the emperor wanted to have surround him "concretely," for the pleasure of immersing himself in an extraordinary place. Literary descriptions merely present the landscape as though it were objective and real. There is an exchange whereby a real landscape becomes a literary one, and the literary landscape becomes a real one, because both are immersed in myth, by virtue of a narrative principle that is always mysterious. The vehicle is the metaphor, a figure of speech associated with mental representation and human language, as well as the objects organized by people.

It is as though we are obsessed with the idea of a universal language expressed through metaphor wherein we are led to believe that nature is eloquent, as Theodor Adorno (1975, 89–112) suggests. We can describe or define a visit or walk through panoramic areas in such a way as to interpret the things around us as a canvas of images that accompany us and correspond to us, forming a cluster of signs analogous to those of language. This experience, a rich flow of patterns and thoughts similar to music, is essentially unreproducible. A nature mediated by the technologies of reproduction risks losing its meaning and value. William Turner and the Impressionists, for example, translated the spirit of the landscape; they did not simply reproduce the landscape. Subjectivity alone could not succeed in defining, in a passive sensory transcription of the world, the pleasure that we feel, as if by enchantment, and which seems to be an enigma. It is the dissolution of the "I" in the imagination that gives us that pleasure. A second moment in the impression tends toward and defines the aesthetic factor. The result of this process is an ability to engage with an object in a contemplative.

Nature appears before our eyes as a true spectacle that invites a keen and absorbed participation: clouds, lightning, patches of sky, stormy seas, and deserts are scenes worthy of Shakespeare, who depicted them in some of his works. From nature's manifestations emanates an ungraspable, ambiguous language consisting of traces or hints that direct us toward secret correspondences. And there are absolutely different ways of describing this experience. We know this from the countless examples in literature and painting, from Friedrich to Corot and Leopardi to Proust. In contemporary literature, the ecstatic gaze has an infinite number of psychological effects that enable us to evoke other landscapes. Marcel Proust was a master of this technique.

When we contemplate, as if we are anonymous protagonists, we experience reality before it is creatively reinterpreted by artists. As Ernst Cassirer has noted, we can stroll through the landscape and feel its charm. We can rejoice in the mildness of the air, the freshness of the fields, the variety and festiveness of the colours, and the fragrance of the flowers. But then we sense a sudden change in our soul. From this moment on, we see the landscape through the eyes of an artist: we begin to paint a picture of what we see. We have entered into a new realm, no longer that of things that exist but that of "living forms." Having abandoned the immediate reality of things, we experience the rhythm of spatial forms, the harmony and contrast of colours, the balance of light and shadow. The aesthetic experience consists of being absorbed by the dynamic aspect of form. Metaphorical language is part of our symbolic thinking and precedes the technical translation of literature and painting.

There is something ancient in this phenomenon. Consider Hadrian's Villa, for example. In the last three centuries, however, our gaze has turned toward the past as though to reappropriate the void left by humankind's separation from nature, which occurred even deeper in the past, and which itself entails a meditation on time. Stimulated in part by scientific studies, an entire world opens up before our eyes, one that crosses the threshold of sense perception and allows us to glimpse the essence of elements that are the foundation of all aesthetic discoveries. However, the catalogue of places and landscapes in this metaphorical discourse on the language of nature is inexhaustible.

As we have seen, the city, too, is landscape. We can leave it and go into nature (as Socrates and Phaedrus did), trading the city for the countryside, but we can also enter the city in order to live among and contemplate its architectural structures. All architecture is landscape and it promotes a relationship in which the human soul learns from the environment. That relationship changes with our landscape, the movements of our gaze, the light, and the seasons. Our eyes and body engage in a contemplation that drifts between the interior and the exterior, between that which is outside and far from us on the one hand, and that which is smaller and within us, unfolding before our eyes, on the other. There is a tight correlation between the aesthetic experience of the natural landscape and that of the urban landscape.

As we discuss this cluster of ideas, I cannot help but think of D'Annunzio, who was equally responsive to the ancient and the modern ("defender of tradition, promoter of modernity"), if we want an example of the creation of a literary landscape. To encounter his veneration of nature, we need only read his *Le laudi del cielo, del mare, della terra, degli eroi* (*In Praise of Sky, Sea, Earth, and Heroes*), his notebooks, his newspaper articles, and the many passages from his works. It is so strong that he achieves a genuine composition of landscape, guided by his poetic skill. This occurs in the Vittoriale. I could consider any number of landscapes as they are depicted by writers. However, I have selected D'Annunzio because in the Vittoriale at Gardone, the poet invents an architecture derived from a vision that fuses reality and artifice, memory and illusion. The garden and the landscape converge to produce an adventure for the eyes. Normally, the sense of adventure does not depend on a before and an after; it is inconsistent or irregular, and does not favour a specific system for observing. At the Vittoriale, however, we find a new and curious fact: a mediated, orderly adventure, such as we might find in a literary text, involving a series of analogies derived from Symbolism and Futurism. It has an aspect that we can call oneiric because it is connected with the imagination. Yet it is also an historical document set within a sort of spatial frenzy. All we need to do is allow ourselves to be swept up by the passage of time as we take in the view from a fixed position, as from any angle of observation, whether in the garden or the park, in order to become aware that we are entering a different dimension of seeing; we are indeed experiencing the beginning of contemplation, but in the way that the poet wanted and planned the project to be read, rather than the way we might decide it should be. Every object stands for another. We are led through a literary garden-architecture-landscape where metaphor reigns supreme. In general, we tend to see fragments, relics of reality, experiences, signs, and memories that come to us recomposed as what seems to be a discontinuous totality. Fragments of history and events, like the ruins of a possessed soul, dominate our meandering gaze.

We find a series of analogies. We are aware of that, in this place, metaphor is the genius of the *Immaginifico* (Creator of Images). The trope is generally understood to mean the use of one word in the place of another for the purpose of creating a referent with different meanings. This entails a semantic transfer based on a relationship of similarity. Basically, one image is replaced by another image or one landscape by another landscape. D'Annunzio imagined the architecture of places in the same way that he imagined the places of architecture.

These are sights at the Vittoriale:

1 The bow of the ship Puglia, an ingenious installation in the garden worthy of a great director, invites us to see before us not a lake but the Adriatic Sea. Indeed, the object is the basis of this type of scenery.
2 One area of the garden appears to be the cathedral of San Giusto in Trieste, facing the great Gulf of Trieste. That particular point encourages remembrance and conjures up a distant place.
3 Due to their terraced structure, the private gardens appear to be in Ravello, which offers visitors one of the most beautiful views of the Mediterranean: a truly exceptional belvedere.
4 The stones from the Carso region of Italy and signs scattered throughout a small green space allowed the poet to relive memories of his heroism, like a giant in a miniaturized geography. This is a dramatic play of distance and proximity that exalts the protagonist.

5 The waterfall, which splits into two streams, may have been
   built following Japanese, Shinto, or Buddhist models (perhaps influenced by the Japanese memorabilia in the priory).
   An important feature is the pathways that lead visitors to
   admire the waterfall, like a framing device that becomes
   increasingly evident.
6 The theatre (or arena) evokes the atmosphere of Magna
   Graecia or ancient Greece, where theatres were a focal point
   from which to appreciate the surrounding panorama. Perhaps this view suggests the one at Taormina in particular.

This illustrates the strategy of quotation and passion for
antiquity we find throughout the work, a strategy saturated
with wartime memories and mythic auras. In this kingdom of
the metaphor, the real landscape, that which lies before us,
becomes part of or makes way for another, that is, an imagined
or evoked landscape. The forms of the real landscape and architecture, including the squares, paths, and gardens, become
actors in a different spectacle, produced by analogy. The literary
landscape, imagined by the poet, becomes an absolutely real
construction, while the real landscape is transformed into an
imaginary one.

The Vittoriale changes its features: the "hermitage" becomes
an isolated, perfumed island, inhabited by the phantasms of
mythology. It becomes an island in the Mediterranean, an ideal
and mysterious Ithaca, but one that is alive and enveloped in the
Greek spirit – a spirit that is, nonetheless, the product of the
principle of contrast, as the poet explains during his voyages.
On a cruise taken in 1895, D'Annunzio writes:

The Greek spirit consists of humankind's continuing reaction to the personality of things. Endowed with such a precise and strong personality, things imposed themselves on
humans. Humans reacted. From this stems the magnificent
personalities of the Greeks – a reaction to things, as the
instinct to dominate. The landscape was exciting. Are not

the trees of the plain themselves, between Patras and Pyrgos, so far from each other, are they not personae? There is a great pine in front of the Museum [of Corinth]. It has a shape and a voice all its own. (1976b, 6, translation by Corrado Federici)

In the Vittoriale, too, we contemplate a clash of personalities – people, the poet, and material objects – and we feel the "Greek spirit" in the air. Indeed, it permeates us. In a passage from his *Taccuini* (*Notebooks*), D'Annunzio states: "Everything here, therefore, is a form of my mind, an aspect of my soul, a manifestation of my fervour" (1976a, 25, translation by Corrado Federici). There is coherence among the themes relating to landscape, like a mental state that gives free reign to the imagination. As visitors, we feel invited, by a strange "daydreaming, to sail in the Mediterranean" (D'Annunzio 1924, 1107, translation by Corrado Federici), propelled by a desire for the sea, woods, and cliffs, and to lie, as he does, in the voluptuousness of being "different and unrecognizable, lost in a solitude full of apparitions and miracles." The Greek spirit of harmonious tension reappears here as controlled intoxication, and so the Vittoriale stimulates dreaming. Looking in the direction of Lake Garda, as though it were a corner of Greece, we feel as if we are looking at the sea dividing Ithaca and Cephalonia. We enter a mythical place superimposed on the objective lake. D'Annunzio describes it in the following way in the same passage from *Taccuini* quoted above:

We are in the classical sea. Great Homeric phantoms rise from every part. We enter the canal. Ithaca is stony, but Cephalonia is rich in vineyards, olive groves, and cypresses. Countless tall, thin cypresses are scattered along the slope and give the entire island a contemplative aspect … I would like to explore the silent island on which the cypresses look like long, thin shadows, like a cemetery. (D'Annunzio 1976a, 39–40, translation by Corrado Federici)

This is daydreaming. How often the poet affirms:

> My life is nothing but a daydream. Dreaming is one thing,
> daydreaming is another. Reality suddenly reveals itself to
> me and approaches me with a sort of imperious violence …
> In an instant, it [reality] dissipates, is deformed, becomes
> transformed, acquires the features of my most intimate
> phantasm. (D'Annunzio 1924, 1104, translation by Corrado
> Federici)

In an imaginary embrace of inner and external vision, the Vittoriale is the product of this ineffable delirium that reshapes landscapes. D'Annunzio situates himself beyond a line, beyond a border that separates two worlds: "From this emerges a feeling of distance and solitude that surrounds me and makes me similar to an island, with no roots" (ibid., 1105, translation by Corrado Federici).

With its bifurcation of meaning, the metaphor invites us to consider the curve and the serpentine line common to baroque style, which in three-dimensional space can take shape as a fold. Gilles Deleuze situates the revival of the historical-stylistic style of baroque in the "enfolding of the soul," which can continue infinitely. Let us leave aside this rhizomatic aspect of Deleuze's thought and get right to the heart of the topic opened up by Deleuze's interpretation of the thought of his interpretation of Leibniz, in which he highlights the concept of a fold that does not lead to an essence, but instead to a function – a space that never ceases to create folds. Indeed, the distinctive feature of the baroque is the fold extending into infinity. At first, the baroque splits the fold, which flows in two directions, as though infinity had two planes: the folds of matter and those of the soul. In this concept, in which matter and spirit are united, unbounded space is visualized as a labyrinth of levels and pathways, straight and curved signs, or lines that bend, creating expansions, bulges, and solids. Leibniz claims that matter, which exists on a lower level, accumulates and is organized in such a way that the parts constitute more or less developed organs that enfold in different ways, while the soul, from its higher level, sings the glory of God as it travels through its own folds without ever finding completion, since these folds multiply to infinity. A multiple labyrinth is the most appropriate diagram to symbolize the inclination of the soul and the curvature of matter because it has many parts, but especially because it is folded in many ways. The soul and matter communicate with each other; in fact, they correspond to each other along the folds. This is how we understand waves, marble veining, oscillation, vibration, and the ceaseless creation of places that fit within other places and disappear within internal folds. The point is always the fold within the fold. We do not see parts divided into parts, lines that are divisible at different points, but rather a labyrinth of continuity that, as with fabric or paper, has an infinite number of folds or is broken up into a curved motion. Folding/unfolding does not so much mean pulling/releasing or contracting/dilating as much as enveloping/developing, involving/evolving. An organism is defined by its capacity to fold its parts infinitely and unfold them to the level of development relative to its species. In this sense, an organism is enveloped in the seed, and seeds are enveloped in one another to infinity (through interlocking embryos). In short, "matter is folded, once under elastic forces, and again under plastic forces" (Deleuze 1992, 10). We are dealing with an irreducible plurality in motion.

There is a theatre of matter that is also a theatre of the spirit. The baroque spirit engages with the body in a complex relationship. Deleuze goes on to say: "Forever indissociable from the body, it [the spirit] discovers a vertiginous animality that gets it tangled in the pleats of matter, but also an organic and cerebral humanity that allows it to rise up and make it ascend over all other folds" (ibid., 11). This is the perennial play of upper and lower levels that entails ascent and descent, and is analogous to the labyrinth of infinite spaces within modern megacities. It is a labyrinth of labyrinths, a map of spaces that fold in on themselves in spiral holographic structures for new areas in which to reside, entertain, organize, and engage in commerce. This play of upper and lower levels results in a distortion of forms that assume the shape of buildings made of strange and shining materials, helipads on the roofs of skyscrapers, and elevated highways that enter urban areas. Are modern megacities, in particular those in Asia and the Emirates, not a baroque reinvention of the urban landscape, with allusions to panoramas of the distant past, yet anticipating *Blade Runner*? Thick decorations, ornaments, and squiggles often mix with the sweat of human labour and the smoke of the new pollutants, while objects and people fly, ascend, and descend in a futuristic scenario that takes on a baroque density and lightness. Matter takes the form of a curve that suggests an imperceptible, airy totality. This is the reformulation of a holistic spectacle that revives the visual play and artifice of the simile. The baroque explored all its possibilities and splendour. Consider the camera obscura, mobile scenic designs, painted backdrops, techniques such as trompe-l'œil applied to walls, secret rooms with no windows – reminiscent of Leibniz's monads – in an interplay of interior-exterior elements: the curios and crowds of figures in the *Studiolo* (private room) of Grand Duke Francesco I de' Medici in the Palazzo Vecchio of Florence, or a church like Sant'Agnese, designed by Borromini with the collaboration of Giovanni Maria Baratta and Carlo Rainaldi, for the Piazza Navona in Rome. These are exaggerated and stimulating elements, machines for creating an extraordinary virtual world through architecture, such as completely incongruous jewellery boxes, impossibly illusionistic skies, and enormous figures imagining the arrival of extraterrestrials. These are the components of the powerful cities of the world at the dawn of the third millennium. Today, we are this delirium.

A fold has no end; we cannot halt the unfolding. It passes through the ceiling, pierces solid objects, and causes bodies to fly. Deleuze presents the idea of imitated or imaginary objects that also become the expression of a second nature, one that tends to create bizarre forms using representational and ornamental devices that are unexpected in the usual sense of representation. This is what he calls artistic genius, which can generate an incalculable number of signs that follow the form of the mathematical line capable of incorporating the infinite potential of a single design curvature: the fold. This is the curve that generates an infinite series of reflections and points of view. The baroque world itself is the infinite curve of curves and points that generates a single variable in a continuous process of unfolding to become a convergent series of all possible series. Like the folds of the soul, the curve and the singularity are the two faces of Leibniz's monad: the atom is a genetic curve. The baroque used a "cryptography" capable of seeing the porous nature of matter and the impalpability of the soul (the enfolding of the soul).

In architecture and in the megacities of today we can see the disquiet of art and nature in an infinite continuum, between the void and fullness, and in the spontaneous unleashing of the imagination, which is capable of offering us a play of distant resonances.

THE CITY, GARDENS, AND LANDSCAPE

In promoting the new and reorganizing the ancient, the contemporary city often relies on the unrestricted invention of forms that are visible in two ways: as part of the general perception of the whole, and the particular relief of the object we want to stand out. In light of the aesthetic canons of the 1900s, which focus on shock, chaos, the exception to the rule, and contrast, all the parts of a built-up area can be interpreted both as background and as specific object. It is the visual and hermeneutical destiny of the work of many architects over the course the last two millennia: a ludic and creative reality. It may be that observers/consumers of the major works in the contemporary urban landscape find it difficult to pick out an object against the background, but it may also be that they find it difficult to pick out the details of the background while their gaze is attracted to a single object emerging against the horizon. We are more or less happy prisoners of the artifice of producing architecture and shaping the city in accordance with a principle of concealment, disguise, and mimesis: the principle of camouflage. A concrete object lies before me, but I am distracted by something that hides it from me. It may be a play of colours or forms, as Bernard Lassus has shown in his analysis of landscape. On the basis of this theory and the process of disambiguation, we can discuss the question of so-called green architecture, buildings with green walls, the new gaze cast on the city in transformation, as well as the relationship among gardens, landscapes, and open spaces.

In addition to the practice of camouflage, Gilles Clément's "third landscape" can be useful to our discussion of urban zones of vegetation. As a reclamation of abandoned and neglected places, hardly cared for by the gardener, and in celebration of wild plants scattered by a wise person who loves a new kind of nature that is not dominated, the third landscape is the landscape of borders and limits between external and internal terrains. The person who contemplates the third landscape is not a fool, but rather the protagonist of an adventure of the gaze and aesthetic taste, one who shifts his or her attention from museums to seek out unnoticed beauty that the wind and light enable to grow in interstices: cracks in rocks, cement, and asphalt. A new urban Jean-Jacques Rousseau who is sensitive to the natural side of a built-up place, he or she aims to make or reorganize, in his or her mind, an art of the city by covering walls and buildings with coats of vegetation. The love of plants and flowers that grow spontaneously elicits profound contemplation; the third landscape is like the third estate, which wields no power and has no power imposed on it. As an analogy to the well-known 1789 pamphlet by Emmanuel Joseph Sieyès, "What Is the Third Estate?" we may pose Clément's question: What is the third landscape? Everything. What has it done until now? Nothing. What does it want to become? Something.

This is an invitation to find a territory-refuge. Let us, therefore, look for this third landscape, find it and preserve it in its simplicity, without mythologizing it. It is difficult not to notice anomalous, sophisticated, artificial elements in the current trend of "green architecture" or "green towns." Why cover walls with greenery or enclose a large window with hundreds of vases of small plants (the atrium of the Kempinski Hotel in Monaco) as though it were a flower shop, while not wondering at all about the meaning of the city, which is quickly exhausting itself, along with its signs and symbols. Consider Thomas Heatherwick's Garden Bridge project on the Thames in London, which connects the Temple tube station with the South Bank. It is a suspended garden on a bridge, and because it is so bizarre it would be an amazing tourist attraction. Perhaps it could be a touch of the new urban picturesque in a London that is losing more and more of its shape. Fashionable objects increase the number of oddities in circulation, but they result from an increasingly superficial planning that has no relationship with either the past or the location.

A different case is Elizabeth Diller's High Line public park in New York, or Jean Nouvel's Musée du quai Branly in Paris, which has a "green wall" created by botanist Patrick Blanc and a horizontal garden by Gilles Clément. A different background and spirit inspired these projects. The first was the product of a community of citizens who wanted to recover an abandoned and degraded industrial area; it was, therefore, a participatory effort, one that has inspired similar interventions in dozens of cities throughout the world. The second is an example of how to bed 15,000 plants on the walls of a museum. With the quai Branly, as in many other buildings of this kind, including those designed by such architects as Kengo Kuma to Edouard François, the critical point is reached in caring for the plants and their growth patterns. In other words, the inhabitant runs the risk of feeling imprisoned in a forest.

Different again are the interventions (and naturalist aesthetics) of Friedensreich Hundertwasser, with his concept of the "tree tenant," and, especially, Terunobu Fujimori with his Grass House in Tokyo. Fujimori's project combines mineral and vegetable elements, a style of Japanese rural architecture featuring bands of vegetation on the roof, and traditional techniques and stylistic innovation from Japan and echoing the 1920s. Within the widespread spirit of "green mania" we can include green towers, such as Edouard François's Tower Flower in Paris, animal sculptures, such as Jeff Koons's *Puppy* (a playful, three-dimensional version of the floral *parterre* [flower bed] in the Guggenheim Museum Bilbao), and terrace gardens on the roofs of skyscrapers.

An unquestioned master of these types of architecture and a true pioneer is Emilio Ambasz. He is an original designer, the creator of the first and most important vertical garden, a man closely linked to the personalities of Amancio Williams and Frank Lloyd Wright, and one of the greats of the last century. Ambasz instituted a dialogue between nature and architecture through a genuinely new theory of the garden. In addition to being an architect and designer, he is also a fine intellectual. What aspect of the creative act does this man, a product of Surrealism, rationalism, and the avant-garde, as well as tradition, pursue? What do his works, especially his architecture, reveal, since they are so pragmatic and yet so mysterious? We might say that imagination and artistic practice come together to give a poetic form to design. How is this possible? It is possible by creating a place of harmony between the natural and the artificial, based on the myth of the gaze at the dawn of civilization. In all his works, Ambasz wants to and succeeds in representing the forms of the marvellous, which is to say, the forms of a primordial, innocent wonder in the face of the objects of the world. He places himself in the mind frame of one who expects to perceive nature as an illuminated entity. The quality of the perception influences technology and the instruments of human endeavour so as to capture this extraordinary moment of an initial understanding of the object, the reality of which derives from an initial inner image.

The material aspect of inventing, representing, and producing objects tends not to free itself of the flash of the initial image, but rather to nurture it: the intentionality of the work consists of the act of preserving the effect of the vision, of that which precedes the word and the sign. In moulding the object in this way, nature continues to illuminate itself through the eyes of the artist, who knows how to learn from fields, flowers, trees, and blades of grass in a constant flow of revelations. In this way, the architect responds to the spirit of the form with which nature reveals itself to us as we contemplate it. It is through intuiting the immateriality of the initial dream image in the materiality of the completed work that we can see the delicate grace of the Casa de Retiro Espiritual (House of Spiritual Retreat) in Seville; the beauty of the building in Fukuoka, a brilliant reworking of the Babylonia ziggurat (Shin-Sanda, in Japanese); and the enigma of the Banca degli Occhi (Eye Bank) in Zelarino, Venice – works designed by Ambasz.

To mould a dream is to give body to the immaterial. This action of shaping, which seeks to transcend what is given to the senses, is the reason for which Ambasz was essentially not directly influenced by postmodernism or deconstruction. Some have called his work technological Arcadia because of its intermediate position. This is certainly a useful term. In this case, however, we need to shift our attention to the doing, the making, and the closeness between creation (*poiesis*) in architecture and creation in poetry or music. With the idea of an illuminated nature, as mentioned above, the analogy of the poet or musician and the architect is apt. The art of building is more than that of a frozen piece of music, fixed in lines and shapes. To give form to a vision by using words, sounds, and signs, or by shaping an object, is part of the same process. It is this doing something well in which an object gives loving attention to its own fantasy, that is, it is beautiful regardless of how it presents itself because nature recalls itself in the image we anticipate, and which we subsequently find made concrete in the work. This is what giving a poetic form to design means.

To walk among these architectural natures and these green structures is the proper way to see and feel the union of intelligence and taste. The aesthetics of the urban landscape is alive in the practice of Pietro Porcinai, in which there is an effective dialogue between exterior and interior. In his works, the nature of the building complies with the model of nature and senses the ambience of each place. The gaze would be enhanced if it could contain the vibrations of Porcinai's creative intention, where nothing is loud or violent. To walk in a city with such images of adherence to nature allows us to embrace the ordinary and impermanent world, but also to free ourselves from it by praising the solitary pathway. The gaze becomes a vibration of forms and figures in a space that is removed from reality and that transforms itself into visions. Those who travel on foot live and act within a network of relationships, both present and concealed, at a rhythmical pace. Only by proceeding slowly is it possible to be in touch with the rhythm of the city. To walk is to poeticize and to philosophize at once. The ancient philosophers enjoyed walking, and this activity is also suited to modern philosophers. It is an experience that invites us to understand the body in relation to the world in a continuous "here and now" that travels in unexplored spaces.

There is another side to the relationship between nature and architecture – namely, the idea of eco-sustainability that some green architecture projects presuppose but do not confuse themselves with because they are focused on construction materials. In this regard there are various interventions by Richard Rogers and Renzo Piano, in addition to the large urban complexes in Stockholm, Freiburg, and Hamburg. Particularly illuminating is Paolo Soleri's experimental town of Arcosanti in Arizona in the 1960s, which illustrates the concept of making various components converge to form a single mass by miniaturizing them. Through emphasizing a reduced rate of exploitation of the environment, and a change in the modes of transportation and transportation systems, and through providing vast areas for agriculture and parks, projects like these propose a model of life that is in harmony with nature. Behind these transformations, events, and experiments is the concept of the "garden city," which came into existence under circumstances similar to those of today, namely, population increase, infrastructure deterioration, pollution, and so on. Ebenezer Howard's intention was to spare the city of congestion and the countryside of abandonment. Letchworth was the first garden city in the early 1900s. Other cities were built in accordance with this model in various parts of Europe, and the idea was revived in the mid-1940s, immediately after the Second World War. The architects and planners of Letchworth Garden City were Raymond Unwin and Lewis Mumford. The 1800s and 1900s saw the spread of community gardens, which were given grants by local governments or non-profit organizations, and which developed in Eastern Europe in particular, but also in Holland, Sweden, and Germany. Historically, the flower and vegetable garden as a defined space in a zone containing biological life in all its species and mutations was very important and was the pride of the Middle Ages, attributed by some to the influence of distant Persian gardens, which were actually more myth than reality. This influence extended to humanism, in the concept of "second nature."

As we have seen, nature is associated with architectural structures. Towns, villages, hamlets, and cities comprise our repertoire as travellers, explorers, warriors, merchants, and walkers. From travel diaries and archives of our collective memory is derived an immense catalogue of the world: the exhilarating wonder of places far and near wrapped in myths, figures, colours, and curios spanning centuries. Observing the urban landscape is part of the aesthetic experience that connects us to nature, because through knowing it and contemplating it, we learn how to interact with our environment. Admiring places like gardens, and other parts of the city and countryside, is really the act of seeing and feeling, but also of perceiving and imagining nature, which presents itself to us in a mosaic of identities. In so doing, nature becomes beautiful because it has the appearance of art, and art, in turn, can be said to be beautiful only when we, aware that it is art, treat it as nature. Art and nature are, in fact, expressions of culture, which, in its long evolution, melds them into a single material and spiritual manifestation, that is, the nature of art, the nature of humankind, the art of things, and the art of life. This is true even when the current epoch seems to be undergoing the death of art, owing to the fragmentation of meaning, the shock effect of media, and the loss of the centre in our doing and representing.

It is important now to comment on the history of the very idea of nature, going back to the year 1000 CE. From the cities of skyscrapers we return to the cities of cathedrals in a rapid overview that will help us understand the stages of artistic heritage, involving philosophy, culture, art, and nature, as has been illustrated. We notice signs of the past when we walk along roads and enter churches, business offices, markets, and government buildings. We look for the spirit of the place in religious and secular buildings from the fourteenth and eleventh centuries, when painting and sculpture were part of architecture and part of the city plan, forming a complete work of art. We enter and exit, going from representations to artifacts and from artifacts to representations, in an engrossing sequence of scripts that acquire and lose their form before our eyes. We walk in the courtyards of civic or royal palaces, gardens, hovels, halls, or cloisters, on whose walls were painted landscapes and towns, then glide down staircases or, hugging walls and fortifications, into squares and the cavernous interiors of churches. It was the age of cathedrals, which we still enjoy dreaming about and reliving as we walk on the ancient pavement, the work of master stonecutters. This was a different world, one of participation, while today everything seems uniform and disconnected. In *Chronicles of the Year 1000*, completed in 1047, Rodulfus Glaber describes urban reconstruction and the people who competed to make projects blossom during a period in which the cathedral emerged as a shining example of the Gothic, a style born in Chartres and Amiens, outside of Italy, and in the original triangular form of the Milan Cathedral, within Italy. We walk past basilicas and palaces, thinking of gardens that have disappeared, the canals, and the cultivated fields outside the city walls. In the eleventh century, Landulf Junior described the beauty of Milan and its gardens as resembling paradise, adorned with trees of different species. And in the romances of the travelling troubadours are descriptions of gardens in small towns or among rustic homes.

I am referring to the poorer Medieval gardens, often built along roads near city walls, next to houses facing the river, but also inside abbeys and courts, as we see in the illuminated manuscript *Les Très Belles Heures de Notre-Dame* (*Turin Book of Hours*) or the *Roman de la rose* (*Romance of the Rose*), and the *Breviario Grimani* (*Grimani Breviary*). These books contain a doctrine of loyalty to nature, a theme written about by Alain de Lille in the twelfth century, as well as a theory of life promoted by William of Conches and Ugo di San Vittore. In this journey into the past, we are surprised especially by Guillaume de Lorris, who in the mid-1200s describes a garden enclosed by walls adorned with allegorical figures, and compares what is depicted with what is real. This is something we find more than two centuries later in Erasmus of Rotterdam's *Familiares Colloquendi Formulæ* (*Familiar Forms of Speaking*). During the Renaissance, alongside the pleasures of living in villas, the pleasures of observing also gain ground, and as a result it becomes almost fashionable to view the forms of gardens and cultivated fields outside the walls from atop towers and palaces: patterns, plants, and rows of trees to traverse, strolling through them with a curious and delighted gaze.

Studies, encounters, and reconstructions/images of antiquity could provide an inspiration for worthwhile projects today, projects capable of recovering an aesthetic and design connection between urban and natural landscapes, despite the current incoherence and fragmentation. At the start of this chapter, I spoke about the importance of valorizing gardens in the city. In light of this, we can perhaps close the wounds inflicted by the expansion of the heterogeneous and the incongruous.

Famous architects such as Mario Cucinella have opened specialized schools that are technical and humanistic in nature, and deal with environmental issues (pollution, use of eco-sustainable materials, and education as it relates to the environment, cultures, energy sources, landscapes, and climate change), with the aim of training "green" innovators in the field of architectural design. This aspect of human activity can be combined with the idea that the city is a text made of stones, a graphic invention, a web of symbols and meanings with grammatical and syntactical elements in a rhetoric of space enlivened by recurring features. As a result, creative labyrinths open up in which we can experience the pleasure of building and living aesthetically, which is also living ethically. What we see always goes together with how we see, and perspectives, feelings, and actions integrate or intersect in a manner that is not disorderly. This is as true for the unfinished or metallic walls of a Le Corbusier or a Gehry, as it is for the vertical grassy carpets of Stefano Boeri's "green towers" or those of the design team WOHA.

A discussion of the relationship between garden architecture, the green city, and the countryside cannot but lead us to deal with the city's exterior and interior boundaries. The areas that have not been built up at the edges of expanding cities are inevitably connected to the empty spaces in the city interior. Reflecting on the urban layout while contemplating a global idea of territory and that which is distant, on the margins, as if it were the centre, is a challenging project and perhaps the only hope for preserving the notion of urban beauty, which we cannot surrender. This is especially true if we observe that the historic centre today is not generally protected by governments. In addition to laxness in the face of deterioration is the indifference (both public and private) associated with the consumption of the patrimony, which leads to abandonment on the one hand, and to the postcard success of a few places selected for their ability to inspire admiration on the other. In reality, the historic centre no longer exists or has almost disappeared. There are banks in the place of cafes, offices in the place of houses, large storefront windows in the place of façades with doors and windows of times past – not to mention the terrain as it relates to traffic and transportation. Thinking of the new city with the spirit of the ancient past can, instead, be the source of a great strategy. It is indeed possible to use that spirit to find a remedy, as Pier Luigi Cervellati has proposed. In the exercise of their profession and role, urban architects take into account the limits of the environment in the face of unlimited development. They move in the opposite direction, veering toward artisanal work and traditional techniques, which are considered to be useful and appropriate for the maintenance of the city and the landscape, thereby showing respect for others' work, as opposed to savagely exploiting natural resources. Attempts are made to restore the original state of ruined places in order to not lose the historical and cultural identity of the space being protected. There are many who restore hamlets, at one time agricultural but now deserted, for the purpose of healing the small and large wounds of the territory outside the city limits, making the passage from the city to the countryside or from the city to the park in the surrounding area less harsh and more gradual.

Finally, in the interest as well of a useful understanding of the relationship between the city and areas of vegetation (flower and vegetable gardens, and cultivated land), we need to be mindful of the struggle against desertification waged by experts. Among the many works of this sort are those of Ibrahim Abouleish and the studies of Pietro Laureano, which have the important objective of introducing biodynamic practices that promote the construction of new oases and the expansion of existing ones. This is to be done so that the earth can continue to flourish and cities can find more than just a kingdom of death all around them. A dose of extreme and impossible measures sometimes makes unattainable hopes credible. Traditional techniques that have educated us for many centuries could guide us once more. We need only observe their results, which include monumental cities in the desert, in order to be convinced. Cesare Brandi describes them so effectively, writing:

> Jerusalem is a city in the desert. Perhaps it did not make this impression on those arriving there from Palestine. They came from the desert and the Jordan is like the final trench in this desert: it suddenly presents the plain of Jericho which produces palm trees, fruits of all kinds … then

a most rugged land appears, one that, although it is not clay, resembles closely the clay of Siena in areas that are harshest and barest … Once again they climb … and climb still. The beautiful walls of Jerusalem, above which appear bell-towers and minarets, the proud dome of the so-called Mosque of Omar, seem to be closed off by the horizon; it suggests something impenetrable. (2002, 114, translation by Corrado Federici)

BORDERS AND MARGINS

Placing ourselves at the city limits and imagining we are living outside, in an out-of-the-way place, walking along the margins, among the buildings of an endless suburb, poised in the midst of buildings, as though in a comic strip or cartoon, is an exciting, thrilling adventure. It is also, however, a way of looking at the city from a certain distance, with both the body and the imagination. Many youths feel and yearn for this pleasure of being physically on the margins, in a neutral zone in which they can roam. This is one meaning of the term "margin," but there are others as well that create a different, strange effect, inside the city itself rather than on its borders. I am referring to the places of the marginalized and the excluded, the new dispossessed people: the new "courts of miracles." When we arrive in Rome and Naples by train or car, from the windows we see figures moving among tiny shacks and makeshift tents on patches of grass near intersections, under bridges, along railroad tracks covered by reeds and wild shrubs mixed with garbage, or along dry drainage ditches. They approach us like unreal human silhouettes with dirty faces, wearing dirty clothes. We are reminded of characters in Victor Hugo's *Hunchback of Notre-Dame*: beggars in the court of miracles. We learn that poverty is still with us, just a few metres away, and that we tend not to be aware of it. What, then, is this feeling of unease and disorientation we get on the train or in the car, we who are the children of affluence and opulence?

We need to ask ourselves what the margins of the city in the age of globalization are. What is expanding and swallowing up the built-up areas, the seat of citizenship? Does a spirit of the city that can give meaning to life for half of the earth's population still exist? What forms do the megacities take in an historical epoch that has chosen to do away with rural culture? These questions concern both the present and the future and are prompted by actions, things, and people as we look for signs of community in transformation. This includes material and immaterial objects, such as the five senses, like taste and food, as well as the traces of the performance and organization of social life. In both its human project and its real dehumanization, the contemporary city is like a cloud of relationships, representations, and actions, but it is also smells and tastes. It is a drifting cloud, which, if its dense particles are studied, displays the spectra of life, infinite forms of work and social dreams, thus highlighting the betrayal of technologies that appear to solve the problems of misery, poverty, and the degradation of people and things. In such a scenario where all problems are solved, we find the cold artificiality of multinationals, to which we can respond only by immersing ourselves in everyday life in order to understand it thoroughly. In other words, we need to use our senses, that is, touch, smell, sight, taste and hearing, to feel the object, namely, the city – both the one that exists and the one that is disappearing, that is, the mutilated, degraded historical city and the one reclaimed by the new wretched of the earth. We need to venture into experience and chance occurrence, observe banality in order to enable awareness to emerge. It is among the most common, obvious things and habits that we find the extraordinary signs of a human race on the move. In the face of this panorama of suffering and desolation, urban planning, with its "scientific" solutions, appears as an abstract system for describing processes. It is based on projects of sustainability and intelligence aimed at understanding the deceptions of the new slavery, upending original good intentions. Touching, feeling, and experiencing life leads us to accentuate the physical world in the face of the digital universe. Faced with the myth of consumerism, we celebrate the value of the creative freedom of the poor, a possible engine for rediscovering a civil relationship.

Today, given rampant speculation on raw materials, environmental catastrophe, and the world energy crisis, the hope of the metropolis rests on a conversation about the humanization of the environment, the battle against exploitation, and the culture of food as a symbolic and real exchange commodity. In light of this, a corporeal politics of public space, especially the anonymous one of non-places, offers examples of active citizenship that involve staying in a place and not merely passing through it. It invites the human sciences to undertake new analytical perspectives outside of abstract interpretation to produce mappings, percentages, probability calculations, and statistics. Rejecting the false promises of "urban prosperity," we should try to capture lived experience so as to observe the way people live, sharing the quotidian – far from the city as finance and the city as spectacle.

With these reflections, I am describing a popular rather than a specialist's vision of the nature of built-up areas and what it could or should be, far from Rem Koolhaas's homologizing fatalism. The life of inhabitants is the basis of a spirit of the shared city, a spirit that engages in the adventure of the limits and the margin. With the phrase "spirit of the shared city," I am trying to emphasize the perception of citizens who wonder about the current forms of urbanization in those places where the senses are diminished or mortified by empty spaces, unfinished projects, stylistic and environmental incongruities, and abandoned areas, either barren or neglected, and at the same time belief in the progress of so-called "architectural genius." We need to keep in mind that in this particular attempt to recover the sense of the city, the big stores and roads are the sites of creative rethinking, including the extreme case of slums as improvised cities. The common spirit is, after all, more than 2,000 years old, because its roots are in urban culture, as described by Mumford: a human experiment in living together in the marketplace, craftsmanship, and art in a dialectic of proximity and passages, in a continuous relationship between people and man-made objects, such as walls, façades, structures of different heights, bridges, and walkways. With the automobile and industrialization, cities have been de-physicalized; they have made places of habitation abstract. Now, in the postmodern global era, which no longer appears to need the countryside or nature, and in which cities are "pure hubs of ubiquity, doorways to a de-materialized geography," as La Cecla contends (2015, 78), this is even more evident. This is the end of the garden city and the idea of inhabitants participating in the design of the city, despite the great effort of Architecture for Humanity. Slogans abound, for example, for smart cities, creative cities, resilient cities, and open source cities. They are a sign of our capacity to create art that can shape the places that we prefer to inhabit.

There is yet another interpretation of borders and margins. It speaks the language of structuralists, deconstructionists, and post-materialists. According to this vision, a mythic aura, persistent myths, and lapsed myths survive in the age of globalization, and new myths remind us of Roland Barthes's analysis from the 1950s and 1960s, and especially of Paul Virilio's recent study.

In the mid-1900s, Jacques Derrida, employing a critique not of the gaze but of creative planning, drew attention to the deconstructive aspect of creative planning, using the notions of text and spatiality, and noting that thinking in the spatial arts can be incorporated into architectural work. Derrida's ideas depart from Heidegger's, although he did set out using the reflections contained in Heidegger's "Building, Dwelling, Thinking" as a starting point. Heidegger, through his ideas on saving the earth, receiving the sky, awaiting the divinities, and taking care of the world, introduced a host of referents to enable readers to apprehend the essence of dwelling, especially in an interval or intermediate place in which to live among things. In contrast, according to Derrida's cultural analysis, we find ourselves historically among fragile inventions and abandoned projects, immersed in a foundation of nothingness that nonetheless produces an aesthetic on the basis of categories unknown until now. Our task is to investigate them. Both Virilio and Derrida read the present beyond modernity, which came to an end along with its distinctive feature, that is, fragmentation. With different objectives, they describe the ubiquitous virtual web, as Tomás Maldonado did. Their views are certainly valid in the West for many reasons, though not always applicable to the Far East. For example, Japanese space, its planning, and its architecture, contains traces of postmodernism and deconstruction. On the other hand, several avant-garde strategies somehow already seem implicit in the traditional art of the Land of the Rising Sun. The notion and experience of an intermediate or liminal space have always contained unstable and de-materializing elements, precisely those in the most recent artistic forms and in western cultural styles. Furthermore, the virtual that Pierre Lévy describes as a synergy of collective intelligence between the virtual/possible and the real/actual – essentially seeing in the virtual world a range of possibilities of the real itself – does not need to be supported by theory in Japan. This is because the country exists in a cultural dimension that is traditionally open to the effects of a future production of computer-generated objects. The point is that the myths of the city and contemporary cultures intersect in the world and create an imaginary space accessible to everyone. Tradition, modernity, and postmodernity interweave to form a spiral that extends across geography and history.

Wishing to express his deconstructive vision, Derrida examined the notion of the *chora* in his discussions with Bernard Tschumi and his collaboration with Peter Eisenman in planning the Parc de la Villette in Paris – a garden of sand and mirrors on multiple levels that was never built. The idea derives from the Platonic *chora* contained in Plato's *Timaeus*. In describing the actions of the demiurge and nature to bring order to the cosmos, Timaeus refers to two kinds of reality, being and becoming, and two kinds of knowledge, intelligence and opinion, as they relate to the invisible model, the visible image, space, and the elements where bodies appear as figures (flat or cubical) and as sensations (smooth or rough). According to this view, sensible forms are copies of intelligible forms. The French philosopher locates the *chora* – space or site – between the two so that every object occupies space and the word assumes logical form. The *chora* is not any known entity, or if we prefer, any entity that is the subject of philosophical discourse, that is, ontological *logos*, which constitutes the law in the *Timaeus*; *chora* is neither "sensible" nor intelligible. Derrida says that the *chora* exists and we can speculate about its *physis* (nature) and its *dynamis* (power or potentiality), at least provisionally, but what is there does not have being. Since all actions, tending as they do toward truth, appeal to generality and a multifaceted order, what we read regarding the *chora* in *Timeaus* perhaps pertains to the "something" that is not a thing. This is because "something" that is not a thing and is not subject to this order in multiplicity ruptures assumptions and distinctions. The referent of *chora*, Derrida goes on to say, does not have the characteristics of an entity that can be accommodated within the ontological sphere, in other words, an intelligible or tangible entity. It is a thing, as I have said, that is not a thing but that persists in its enigmatic uniqueness without allowing itself to be seen, visualized, or determined. Deprived of its real referent, it has nothing of its own and remains formless (*amorphon*). Such an unusual lack of properties (indeed, it is nothing) is precisely what the *chora* must retain, so to speak – what must be retained for it, and what we must retain for it. The *chora* does not receive (as a receptacle) for itself; therefore it must not receive, it must only allow itself to borrow the properties of what it receives. Is this "mode" unique or typical? Does it contain the uniqueness of an everyday event or the normalized generality of a paradigm? Stated differently, and staying within the discussion of the idea of the boundaries separating things, names, and spaces, the *chora* receives all these properties in order to give them place, but does not possess any of them itself. It "is" nothing other than the sum or process of that which is to be inscribed "on" it, regarding its subject, although it is not the *subject* or the *supporting presence* of all the properties attributed to it, but to which it is not reducible. Very simply, this surplus is nothing – nothing that is or can be said to exist ontologically. This absence of support, which cannot be translated as absent support or absence with regard to support, gives rise to and resists all definitions (binary or dialectical) and all philosophical – and more rigorously, ontological – crystallizations.

The expression "give place" does not refer to a gesture on the part of the subject giving support or origin to something that is given to someone. As well, the "figures" it proposes in relation to the cosmos are not even real "figures." Philosophy cannot speak directly about that which those figures indicate, the modes of vigilance or truth (true or probable). The *Timaeus* calls this "thing," which is not anything it seems to be, *chora* (location, place, space, dwelling). It is, however, a "giving place"; it does not pertain to ideal paradigms of things or to copies of things. It is neither sensible nor intelligible, neither metaphor nor literal, neither this nor that; it participates and does not participate in the two terms of the binary. *Chora* is also called "matrix" or "nurse." Ungraspable and elusive, it invites us to go beyond origin to understand difference and the form of access, as well as the space that receives it. It is an interstitial space in our thinking and doing, a place within a hypothetical future democracy that transcends and deconstructs every *nomos* (law or custom) on earth. In other words, it goes beyond the norms that instituted political space via a concrete act of differentiations, as Carl Schmitt (2003) would say. We find ourselves, therefore, beyond the acquisition of a portion of land, beyond the portion provided by a measurement that goes beyond itself to create a "political" space of belonging or ownership. Through Derrida, a reader of the *Timaeus* can explore the possibilities of the limit, prior to the *nomos* of the earth and in strict connection with the earth via human settlement, prior to the division of space into a place selected by people on which to build their homes and to establish a system of exploitation of natural resources. Only in this way can we see how the divided space can become a shared space, an space of participation, the "*chora* of the political." I have in mind the non-places of those who have no rights or property, the wretched of the earth, which we find outside and inside the city. How do we measure, with the wretched, the *nomos* of the earth? In this view of the hell of the limits of dwelling and living, there is, despite everything, a force for human regrouping that transcends negativity, allowing this condition to change into hope – as we glean from Arjun Appadurai, who discusses a strategy of the social imaginary that in the near future would see poverty as a form of negotiation between individuals. In essence, an ethics of possibilities revolving around the theme discussed above, namely, the *chora* of the political, emerges.

Still on the question of the going beyond, this moving toward a place with no foundation and that precedes the *nomos*, we could consider another useful idea of Heidegger's from the early 1960s, one that shifts attention away from the theory of representation to the dynamics of the void. He discusses the concept in relation to sculpture, but we can also apply it to the form of the city as an immense sculpture of the habitat. In *Art and Space*, the German philosopher states that the void is usually understood as the lack of that which fills empty spaces and interstices. However, it is also related to that which is proper to place, and for this reason it cannot be considered a lack but rather an "unconcealment." According to Heidegger, the void is nothing; it is not even lack. In being embodied in sculpture, the void plays a role in the way places are instituted, enriching and holding them open. Sculpture is an embodiment of the truth of being in its instituting places (an initial observation of that which is proper to this art reveals the fact that its truth is not necessarily embodied). He concludes his discussion by quoting Goethe, for whom it is not always necessary for the truth to be embodied; rather, it suffices that it drift in the vicinity like a spirit and inspire a kind of accord, "as when the sound of the bells drifts as a friend in the air and as bearer of peace" (Heidegger 1988, 271).

The borders and margins of the things and horizons around us have led us to concentrate on the in-between place. This is not a modern problem, but an ancient one. As Dario Del Corno reminded me some years ago, that which is external cannot be read according to that which is called *chora*. In its original meaning, the Greek noun *chora* indicates a definite space, which can refer to a territory or a place as location. In addition to this general designation, there is specific meaning that relates to the countryside as opposed to the city, to which the *chora* relates as an integral part of a whole. In that long conversation, as I recall, Del Corno described how, in the solemn proem of the oration *Against Leocrates*, the Athenian orator Lycurgus invoked the statues of the gods and heroes springing up in the cities and the Attic *chora*, thus clarifying both the difference and the complementarity of the two spatial models. Aristotle (1959, 3, 31–2, 1283a) then defines the *chora* as a "collective possession" in the sense that every citizen can participate in it. Passages by Thucydides (II, 5, 7) and Xenophon (III, 6, 11–12) confirm that *chora* referred expressly to the contiguous zone of the city reserved for agricultural production. In the current urban situation, we have discovered the extreme form of these kinds of borderlands.

PHYSIOGNOMIES OF EMOTION

When we perceive the features of a place, which borders and margins appear to us if we take into account the artistic translation of the physiognomies of emotion, as though these features were one of its forms of expression? Can emotional reactions cause the morphology of a landscape or a city to change? Mental states involving an immediate psychological response seem to play a role in a sort of correspondence. Between the subject and the object, what is the boundary of the image when it becomes a mental representation of the natural object? The emotions blur like physiognomies. Precision is lost in the pleasure of the fantasy, which reconstructs reality and takes it to be concrete. This is true especially in the case of photography, cinema, and virtual technologies, which have become the prostheses of the senses and which create the illusion that simulations are reality.

Emotions alter the images of the city; historically, they are like an inner and affective form or design tied to first representations. It is known that in the western tradition, design is the father of all the arts. This is true for Vasari, as it is for da Vinci, Raphael, and Michelangelo. "Disegno" is a founding idea or essence that structures representation; it concerns both images and things – all of nature is contained in it. Erwin Panofsky has dealt skilfully with design in this sense. He describes how it retains experience and all emotion in a grand orchestration of signs: it illustrates, describes, projects, and visualizes the entire world. In the immediacy of an impression and an emotion, the city is also, essentially, a design, the product of a vision and imitation, the work of forms and traces, an image of masses and surfaces, the art of planning and of technology, a creative whole or wondrous *poiesis* that can be enclosed within a design that is at once practical and ideal. All the haphazard doing and building that humankind was able to produce over three millennia was given order or organized structure. From the ancient Greek and Roman model to that of the Renaissance, up to the 1800s, the city is the result of a poietic conceptualization, that is to say, an explicit form that responds to an implicit one in a representational mirroring.

For more than a century, however, design has been devalued, the idea has lost its centre, and civilization is undergoing a crisis of its symbolic function. The structure that held the city together around an idea, despite its composite nature, has split apart as practices, technologies, languages, and habits have undone the whole, which now flows in a thousand external rivulets that empty it of its sense and give rise to a new, improvised, anonymous, and confused growth. Thus, the city expands into the chaos and haphazardness that prevail. In the age of technical reproduction, fragmentation, contradiction, and incoherence are favoured. We see their effects in the arts of photography and cinema, as well as in those that produce virtual reality. The city has been affected by these changes, in plans for its expansion, the style of architecture, and the quality of life and dwelling, as well as the sensibility it has promoted. Particularly in the 1930s, the avant-garde and modernist movements in architecture reflected the loss of the aura and the contemplative aspect of art, and in the context of the new rationality, focused their attention on an urban planning that revolved around the Athens Charter, a much-discussed document that attempted to define the modern city while offering useful suggestions on living and dwelling in the world. The emergence of the new, the shocking, and the provocative corresponds to the end of cultural representation. Weber, Simmel, Kracauer, Benjamin, Heidegger, Lukács, and Adorno interpreted the state of the city in the course of an epochal, profound change and provided an entire imaginary that, in pre-Second World War cinema, revolved around Fritz Lang's *Metropolis* and Charlie Chaplin's *Modern Times*, and more recently has given us such films as *Brazil*, *Batman*, *Matrix*, *Star Trek: Enterprise*, *I Am Legend*, *Inception*, *Skyfall*, and *She*. To our mind, the futurisms of cinema and comic strips fuse together as real visions of the megacity. We fall into the trap of optical illusion. The big object that excites us is the skyscraper, with its dizzying height. It represents the new wonder of the world, and we move from cathedrals to skyscrapers. Which do we choose: William F. Lamb's classic Empire State Building (New York, 1931), Skidmore Owings's Sears Tower (Chicago, 1974), Cesar Pelli's Petronas Towers (Kuala Lumpur, 1998), Adrian Smith's Burj Khalifa (Dubai, 2010), Kohn Pedersen Fox's Ping An International Finance Centre (Shenzhen, 2010), or Terry Farrell's China Zun (Beijing, begun in 2011)? This, without omitting the clever oddities of Rem Koolhaas (the CCTV, Beijing, 2010) or those of Renzo Piano (the Shard, London, 2012). The cinematic and virtual imaginary has changed the state of the symbolic; in the age of globalization, the new tower unites language rather than divides it, thereby promoting incomprehension among peoples. It is not cinema and the city that I want to discuss; I would, instead, like to examine the perception of the urban territory – a more up-to-date and appropriate term that underscores the broad physiognomy of the spatial emotions – and thus get to the heart of a description of the suffering that is a part of dwelling and moving about in the city.

In this book, I do not discuss the visual dynamism of a Dziga Vertov or a Walter Ruttmann, the stark realism of Lionel Rogosin's *On the Bowery*, or the nostalgic or "pathetic" vision of a Pier Paolo Pasolini or Wim Wenders.

Social space and individual space meet in our gaze and together shape reality, sometimes in harmonious ways, often in conflicting ways. Built-up space becomes a metaphor, a narrative of pathways and maps involving a rhetoric of dwelling, moving, and walking whereby we can draw a certain analogy between figures of speech and pedestrian walkways. The expressiveness and the physicality of movements are allusive and fragmentary. This is a non-linear strolling that makes reading and interpreting the whole waver: solid masses of architecture, roads, horizontal and vertical routes (taken inadvertently or intentionally), signs and graffiti on walls. This is all a game of losing and finding ourselves in anthropological space, between the material and the immaterial, as we create a poetic narrative. Visiting, living, and moving about are part of the new dimension of the urban landscape. In the last four decades, with the celebration of the hybrid, the eccentric, and the discontinuous, theories have come from different philosophers and anthropologists, such as Foucault, Baudrillard, Deleuze, de Certeau, Augé, Virilio, Derrida, Bauman, and La Cecla. Long gone are the days of Roman Ingarden (1962, § 291), who in the final phase of modernism, in speaking about the ontology of art, called architecture a *constructive* process in that it is pure music relative to the other arts. This is because architecture is capable of creating new forms that include irregular and heterogeneous elements, even as it idealizes and materializes. The product of the coexistence and integration of humankind and nature, it is an organic reality, in that out of apparent ambivalence comes a complex set of abstractions, properties, and stylizations in which roles and functions construct unforeseen environments.

From modernism we moved to postmodernism toward the late 1900s, and from constructivism to deconstruction. But also far from all this, as part of a process of constant obsolescence, is the current fashion of an "excited society" given over to sensationalism, about which Christoph Turcke writes, and before him Reinhard Schulze. In our frame of reference, it is no longer a question of capturing the extraordinary but rather the features of a morphology of emotion, something intimate and troubling in human life, in design that is disfigured everywhere in the modern city and in the lived experiences of its inhabitants. Walking, feeling, and communicating interweave to wrap the inhabitant in symbolic meaning, such as the gestures of living as they appear in the films of Iranian director Amir Naderi or those of Danish director Nicolas Winding Refn. Forms and images, minds and hearts that appear to change both in the global city, as Saskia Sassen has shown, and in the networked city, according to Manuel Castells. In the urban void there is a tendency to give a new face to familiar and consumed space. The space we see and inhabit becomes another space; at times it feels like a diseased organism, as do we who are part of it. I need to clarify that it is not the city of drugs and alcohol that Spike Lee depicts or the seemingly sterile city in Francis Ford Coppola's *The Conversation* that is of interest to me here. Also not pertinent here is the psychological dimension of Mathieu Kassovitz's *The Hate* and the *banlieue* (French suburbs) films of the 1990s. In Naderi's trilogy we observe the metamorphosis of characters interspersed among empty frames. The film is a series of images that flow freely as though by improvisation: subways, walls, underpasses, nightclubs, parks, people, etc., in a science fiction atmosphere that conflates fiction, reality, unreality, and virtuality in an engaging but incoherent quest, as in all adventures of this description.

In the landscapes of the global city, we also find the imagination of Winding Refn. Corporeality and madness shape the space by presenting underground scenarios of violence and inhumanity in a context of inequality and social imbalance. There is a certain mirroring effect or sense of shared reality between people and places: we appear as fearing subjects and consumers of goods in a space that tends constantly toward the incomplete and indistinct. The image is not fixed or specific but rather drifting and elusive, giving rise to new forms of mobility or atmospheres, as though suspended in time. The web of circulation and communication expands and becomes denser while the disorienting feeling that the entire visible world is being urbanized takes hold. From this comes the idea of a globalizing consciousness that causes things that are crude, threatening, squalid, dirty, and criminal to emerge: something pathological produced in a post-Tarantino hyper-real style.

The representations of the city in the films of Godfrey Reggio shed light on a different aspect, that of the morphology of the natural object as it undergoes transformation as a result of the passage of time and human presence. Territory subjected to human work and devastation changes its appearance and turns into a city. This is communicated in his films through powerful images that portray an enormous tragedy. Geology merges with aesthetics to offer sublime hints of that which cannot be measured, which the film emphasizes through the massive natural phenomena captured by the moving camera/gaze. The dizzying speed of the editing makes it seem as if the physical landscape is being devoured from the inside. With its effects, the film renders explicit and clear the word *koyaanisqatsi*, which means "life out of balance" in the Hopi language. Civilization transcends nature, splitting it in two to reveal a profound change in life situations. The image fuels itself and reopens the ancient debate on the question of *natura naturans* and *natura naturata*. People and things appear to be separate and united at the same time. In this perspective of relativity and difference, nature appears to be "naturing" in people, both the artist who works by transforming it and the observer who loses himself or herself in the process of perceiving and contemplating it. People rediscover in themselves the power of that original and formless plasma that is the evolving world. Nature, art, and culture thus interweave in the physiognomies of emotion, which the films of Reggio portray and celebrate.

We live in the age of multifunctional cell phones. How do the physiognomies of emotion relate to a new *flânerie* in the megacity? Do our minds and bodies still feel the thrill that Benjamin (2000, 46) described when we walk around carrying a cell phone? We seem to have lost the pleasure of walking and stopping to look at windows and things around us, pausing at intersections and in cafes. We do not allow ourselves to be drawn to people and crowds. Are we still participating when we go into the throng of people that envelops us at a bus or train station, or in Tokyo's Shibuya square, or when we walk along the Great Wall of China or enter the Forbidden City in Beijing? Crowds are different: those of New York City are anonymous and not fussy, while those of New Delhi are like a fragrant giant in motion. Cell phones take us to a realm of aesthetic indifference, located between the real and the virtual. We do not apprehend the world around us and are deaf to the latent spirit of events. We are distracted. As postmodern people, we have an air of detachment and superiority with respect to the world. Strolling is educational and something of a ritual, but today the typical figure of modernity, the *flâneur*, who is now identified with the tourist or the idler, does not practise ludic hedonism. They do not linger or pretend to linger in the world and with the people around them. The melancholy wanderer no longer lets himself or herself go, having lost the innocence that was once complicit in a way with external reality, and shut off any pretentions of being interested in a place or thing. The sophisticated art of solitary and melancholy lingering has faded, as has the freedom that goes with it. As Giampaolo Nuvolati (2013, 9) explains, the *cyber-flâneur*, who denies the value of the classic *flâneur* by collapsing the public and the private spheres into vacuity, is gaining ground. The somewhat snobbish taste of the figure who prefers the margins, rejecting plans and groups of people, is coming to an end. The solitary dandy, perhaps limited in resources, sees the world of consumers and the lights of the marketplace, but does not involve himself or herself very much in it. The *flânerie* that was also *rêverie* (daydream), the pleasure of seeing and imagining places, gardens, buildings – all the while evoking the atmosphere of ages past – is dying. And yet, because it was a modernist practice in the age of the metropolis, why could it not be preserved in postmodern society in the age of the megacity? *Flânerie* old and new are like art forms in recent decades: we can think of the *flâneur* as the collective subject who intervenes in the environment, privileging urban, marginal voids and abandoned spaces. He or she is the guide and artist in the disquieting, changeable, and confused world of borderlands. We can also imagine him or her as a hybrid figure who, cell phone in hand, rummages around, like someone searching for what is discarded and overlooked, though maintains contact with the world of the internet, for the purpose of surfing in the cyber-mass as though it were a jewel of the entertainment and communications society.

As Siegfried Kracauer noted, even in the postmodern epoch, looking back at the modern period of 1927, visible manifestations (in the sense of not being clarified by the conscious mind) guarantee immediate access to the thing at hand, knowledge of which, conversely, is tied to its interpretation. The fundamental content of an epoch and its undetected impulses illuminate each other. *Post-metropolitan flâneurs* can find their own strategies of absence and the void, both of which are expressible in aesthetic terms. Masses are revealed to be a myth or an abstraction – that is to say, reality is merely an appearance that this configuration assumes when compared to representations of things that are concrete. In fact, it is the crass manifestation of nature, dissociated from its most genuine value, on its lowest level. Nature has more play when the capitalist *ratio* is freed of every restriction and, ignoring people, dissolves into the empty abstractness from which it emerges. The contemporary *flâneur* is indeed the interpreter of the postmodern scene, a typical symbol of the erasure of human essence.

His or her movements, seductions, and attitudes construct places that are always different and new. He or she is not yet a doppelganger, a robot, or a clone. Postmodernism offers up the image of a new urban *promeneur* (stroller). A stranger at home and familiar to strangers, he or she still expresses emotions, in spite of being imprisoned by the iPhone. This figure perhaps exercises a mental *flânerie* in an ever-increasing solitude in the metropolis in the face of a dizzying play of anthropomorphic images, strolling along streets that look like veins, old walls with enormous shoulders, and parks that look like lungs. He or she lives in a city that is far removed from the *polis* and all that it stands for, but definitely has not lost the desire to be among ancient walls that exude myth and grace. Lost in nostalgia, however, he or she might say with Pindar, in an attempt to revive it:

O shining and violet-crowned and celebrated in song,
bulwark of Hellas,
famous Athens, divine citadel.
("Dithyramb for the Athenians," fragment 76)

3

The Art of the City

BEAUTY AND BUILDING STEREOTYPE

In the preceding pages, we have attempted to understand what the city is and how it appears historically and culturally. We have examined some fundamental aspects of its images and meanings over the course of civilization. We have reflected on its nature, form, and capacity to build, imagine, and inspire. We have described the domains of representation and emotion, and considered its symbols, limits, and paradoxes. Does an art of the city actually exist, and if so, in what does it consist? This question is implicit in the discussion of the preceding pages. We now need to now take up the issue in a more direct fashion. In other words, we need to establish the reasons for its beauty, and at the same time examine the notion of building stereotype. In other words, we need to ask ourselves what the difference is between routine and creativity.

The art of the city is a collective art in that it expresses the culture incorporated in a place in order to create other places that are considered more comfortable; it transforms nature, from which it draws its resources, and entails thought that facilitates building on the earth, using its physical laws. Indeed, architecture shapes immense sections of the environment. Through the sum of the its architectural structure and habits, the product of work, perception, and the organization of life, the city unleashes the capacity to produce great works and gives the world an art that, based on history, represents enormous human effort and daring. In his *Pensieri diversi* (*Thoughts*) (1980, 87, translation by Corrado Federici), Ludwig Wittgenstein states: "Architecture is a gesture. Not every purposive movement of the human body is a gesture, just as not every functional building is architecture." This image of the gesture of architecture that is created in physical space is relevant and interesting because it establishes a relationship between the individual and urban society. In addition, we have here a practical illustration of the imagination at work. It is precisely to highlight this living and active form that Gilles Deleuze, in explaining the notion of the fold in various parts of his study of Leibniz and the baroque (1992), claims that architecture does not begin with the flesh but with the house, and that it is first among the arts. In fact, the forms of architecture, even the most refined, always construct and join together levels and borders. In addition to suggesting movement, architecture is a "cornice" (or set of interlocking cornices facing in different directions) that imposes itself on the other arts, from painting to cinema. In these pages, I will not be discussing the pathological state of modern cities, but rather the fact that the city resides between philosophy – which originated with the creation of the concepts of immanence, friendship, and opinion – and the history of contingency, in the form of continual de-territorialization that begins with nomadic or sedentary societies. In this case, the city is a network or system of circulating ideas and things that come into existence and pass out of existence.

To provide greater detail on the notion of the art of the city, it is useful to take into account ideas from eighteenth-century France, documented in the *Encyclopédie* (*Encyclopedia*). In particular, we can refer to the ideas of Denis Diderot (see the entries for *art* and *artisan*), who, rather than reiterating the discussion on the major or minor guilds, which were in their heyday during his lifetime, introduced a great social idea for the progress and future of human activity. In his definitions, Diderot chooses to swim against the current, defining the artist in terms contrary to the rigid distinction between the liberal and the mechanical arts, and between intellectual work and manual labour. He applies the term to someone who exercises either an art or a science that presupposes a level of intelligence, the difference with respect to the work of an artisan being the hierarchy of the guilds (intellectual work, manual labour) and the different kinds of intellectual work that the guilds perform. Art, therefore, is not so much an expression of the prestige deriving from the aesthetic value of the fine arts, as it is a social and intellectual reassessment of work and technique. This concept is along the lines of the ideas held by Bacon, in which the trades and scientific work were elevated for their psychology of inventiveness and development of production capacity. In this context of activity and industriousness I present my own comments on architecture and the city, which relate to the realms of rules and abstractions, realms that contribute to the greatness of humankind. As Diderot might say, experimental and applied geometry is assisted by pure geometry. The following is his advice:

> An individual should leave the academy and go down into the laboratory to see the phenomena of the guilds so he may describe them in a work that induces artists to read, philosophers to think in useful terms, and the powerful to make good use of their authority and their recompense. (Diderot 1988, 96, translation by Corrado Federici)

Artists and intellectuals, therefore, making full use of their intelligence and implements, should promote the well-being of society. Diderot encourages them to conduct experiments together, since humanity has always dominated and interpreted nature; the arts, technologies, and sciences should proceed in unison. On the one hand, there are technical rules according to which an object is produced; on the other hand, observations can be made from various points of view. We engage in both a practice and a theory. As Diderot goes on to say, implements and rules are like muscles, complementing those of the arm, and acting as accessories for the intellect. What the French philosopher says about art (ironically in the eighteenth century, when the metropolises were forming) is especially useful for our reflections on the city, and on its industriousness and idealism in building and imagining. In this sense, real beauty sheds light on the megacities of today. By real beauty, I mean the perception of relationships and combinations in a mesh of images that break through the limits of space and time while avoiding the dangers of the modernist style, which can produce monotony. We must always safeguard the genius of invention. Thus, Diderot anticipates the era of design and applied arts.

There is an entire history of beauty that we need to examine: both that of antiquity and modernity.

The ancient world is revisited in an interesting way in the 1900s. I am referring to Paul Valéry's *Eupalinos, or The Architect*, published around 1920 as a preface to *Album Architectures*. The poet reinvents a Platonic dialogue to show that an idea and the search for the truth tend toward the analysis and construction of form. He reminds us of the rules of Eupalinos of Megara in order to affirm the desire that human creations be eternal. What is the relationship between knowing and building? Is knowledge of ideas related to the search for and creation of forms? The text revolves around a poetics of knowledge. In Valéry's interpretation, architecture is the art that seeks perfection and harmony, which makes it similar to music. Like music, architecture goes beyond imitation, because it is not enough to imitate nature to achieve a perfect creation. The two have numbers and geometric rhythm in common. In this dialogue, we find two precepts: "Il n'y a point de détails dans l'exécution" (In execution, there are no details) and "Il faut que mon temple meuve les hommes comme les meut l'objet aimé" (My temple must move people as a cherished object moves them). In the second precept, we infer enchantment, such as the passion for forms and appearances. Furthermore, we notice that there are silent buildings that speak and sing. Stones evoke the history of a place and its people; they sing as a result of their capacity to rise against the pull of gravity, as Amphion tells it, or they are silent as a result of their mysteriousness.

Natural objects are juxtaposed with man-made objects, which are subdivided into useful and beautiful objects. The point in Valéry's text that pertains to our discussion is that artwork offers itself to our attention like a practical, analytical object, and as a product of calculation, experience, and technical skill. In addition, the form of an artwork, based on a model provided by architecture or music, must always refer to something else by analogy, in accordance with the process typical of these arts. In fact, the arts are recognizable as such because of their capacity for adhering to universal laws that, ironically, they apply to underscore their inner will to affirm their aesthetic value. These ideas are important for our discussion on the composite nature of architecture and the city.

We are referring to the concept of beauty as a value, as Cacciari (2004, 73–5) asserts. All the forms of the city, which were at one time different, seem to be caught up in a process of homologization, whereby their aura dissolves. Our historical cities are becoming institutions of remembrance; they are turning into museums. Furthermore, the idea and practice of dwelling is a concern for an entire set of urban planning problems relating to beauty, a term that is increasingly ambiguous. Today, in fact, when we refer to beauty, we apply it strictly to the aesthetic aspect of what we like and find pleasurable. In the classical world, beauty came with a broad spectrum of characteristics, indicating something well formed, well articulated, well built, and durable, adhering to the canons – that is, a *logos* that transcends the individual works. It was more of an objective category than a subjective one. How can our cities, then, express the indefinable quality of the life of citizens through the sum of its buildings? Cacciari believes that city-territories are the homeland of *varietas* (variety), the artificial, the anti-canonical, and that we should pursue a special *varietas* combined with *concinnitas* (harmonious balance), a notion that, though classical, allows for a range of forms, such as the heterogeneous modulation of aspects of a structure. It would be worthwhile to experiment with this concept once again.

We can also approach the question of beauty from a sociological perspective. When beauty was paired with functionality in the 1920s and 1930s with the avant-gardes and the innovations of the Bauhaus of the Weimar Republic, the problem was raised of the relationship between industry, modernism, and design. In an essay from the mid-1960s, Adorno (2008, 170) addressed this problem and analyzed it in light of aesthetics. Architecture, too, reflects "the dual nature of art," that is, its autonomy and social aspect, but it can also be part of a utopian project. Due to its formal norms, architecture also contains the negation of the society in which it operates; the degree of its autonomy determines its value. In this way, it avoids ideological and acritical conformity. Adorno writes:

> Beauty today can have no other measure except the depth to which a work resolves contradictions. A work must cut through the contradictions and overcome them, not by covering them up, but by pursuing them. Mere formal beauty, whatever that might be, is empty and meaningless; the beauty of its content is lost in the pre-artistic sensual pleasure of the observer. (1997, 17)

According to Adorno, beauty is the product of a "resultant of force vectors," and aesthetic thought today, though it concerns itself with art, must no longer see beauty as its correlative. Beauty must, instead, surpass art itself, surpass the outmoded opposition between that which is purpose-oriented and that which is not, an opposition under which the creator suffers as much as the observer.

At this point of our discussion of the beautiful city and its crisis of identity, we should reflect on restoration and building stereotype. This involves conservation and memory, which involves the principles of equilibrium, symmetry, and decorum, and the canons of western classical aesthetic taste, expressed through the centuries. This aesthetic saw the structure of the historic centre as a unique monument, subject to a number of stylistic and historical superimpositions. I am not referring to the spread of *kitsch* in the period following the Second World War, but to the technologies applied to purpose-oriented crafts. For this reason, building stereotype is related to restoration. The latter concerns the traditions of artisans and the materials used (stone, brick, wood), taking into consideration not only the ideas of Viollet-le-Duc and John Ruskin on the restoration and contemplation of architectural forms of the past, but also the techniques that have continued to be applied for centuries and millennia. Pier Luigi Cervellati (1991, 71) describes the question of the beauty of buildings and their restoration. He also sees restoration as being connected with materials and architectural stereotypes in an age in which urbanism is driven by an ideology of consumption, bringing the industrial age to a close. More has been built over the last fifty years than in the 5,000 years prior, and both the human habitat and building models have deteriorated. In the contemporary age, we are in need of a restoration practice that can be either urban or environmental. According to Cervellati, the philosophy of restoration is the same, which is say, whether we are restoring the features of a building, an area of the city, or the environment, or attempting to achieve a certain equilibrium among the parts when it is not possible to recover the original form. It is not so much a question of restoring the original features as restoring the equilibrium that the form had prior to being altered.

Let us now discuss modernity. I will not discuss Le Corbusier, since much has already been written about him and his great, modern, functionalist architectural projects. Instead, I will discuss Kenzō Tange, who is less well-known in Europe, and some visual, symbolic, and material stereotypes that he applies: images of nature and architectural clichés.

Understanding Kenzō Tange's architectural poetics – that is, his design ideal of using technologies that allow him to build without damaging the beauty of the land – requires an initial observation of the Japanese landscape and its decline. Destroyed for the most part across the centuries by earthquakes, and more recently the bombardments of the Second World War, as well as by post-industrial exploitation, the Japanese landscape continues to be a mystery to behold. What remains of it and its heart-rending transformation reveals fragments of a world that, if observed closely, still manages to unite history and mythology, as well as creative planning and oneiric vision. This is because in the Land of the Rising Sun, citizens do not deny the power of dreams, even after unspeakable devastation. The flow of innovation is an integral part of traditions that move unseen beneath the frenzy of incessant change. Despite terrible and tragic upheavals, nature, including human nature, really seems to dream in this country, like the reclining Buddha who, in the state of nirvana, looks out on a perplexed or weeping humanity with an enigmatic smile on his lips. This is an image that recurs in painting and sculpture like an archetype of the collective imaginary. It is found everywhere. An image of disaster and the sublime, and the actual and the imagined landscape, associated with a dream of regeneration, are indissolubly fused. From the gardens of Kyoto to the sacred mountains, from the temples to the performances of *Noh* theatre, and from the *haiku* to the traditional home, lived in as though it were "an empire of signs," as Roland Barthes might say, we sense the survival of a play of extraordinary gazes and a flowering of unexpected "transcendences." The relationship between the world, sky, and paradise is present everywhere; prompted by the variable beauty of the cosmos and the spirit, the aesthetic model becomes a model for ecstatic experience or vivid, enlightened contemplation. We might say that between experience with the symbolic and evidence of emptiness, both the truth of things and a creative output emerges. Everything we look at looks at us. The ordinary nurtures the extraordinary. Tange's experience begins with this, the art of the traditional Japanese landscape and its disfigurement in the contemporary age, and the fluid universe of *satori* (understanding) or humankind's awakening to nature itself. In his work, imagination is grounded in tradition, as Tange himself acknowledges in his early writings. In our study of the forms of the art of the landscape and the art of the city, we should bear in mind what

Barthes said about Tokyo. He referred to it as a city with an empty centre. The entire city revolves around a site that is, in Barthes's words, prohibited and indifferent, a residence concealed beneath foliage, protected by moats, and inhabited by an emperor who is never seen. This centre is like an evaporated ideal that is not meant to emit any kind of power but instead offers its own emptiness to all urban movement as a form of support, something concentric and fluid. We must remember, too, that the traditional Japanese house revolves around this evanescent identity. In this way, the imaginary unfurls in endless circles around an empty core. This is the general sense of the observations I am about to make on Tange's work.

In Japanese art of the last century, with its incorporation of western "isms" associated with the avant-gardes, we see that signs of tradition and traces of the ancient past are often not abandoned or lost but hidden in essential forms. In architecture, even where at first sight we might not suspect any continuity with the past, and instead expect contrast or deviation from its aesthetic lessons, traditional culture survives. It does so in traces, it is true, but still it reveals itself. Among the architects working in a period in which the landscape is greatly disfigured, especially from the Second World War to today, Tange stands out not only for his daring, innovative, modern solutions but for his tendency to somehow preserve traditional inspiration as well. He belongs to the transitional generation that sought to transform the city itself into a "utopia" by following the artistic thinking of the 1900s, which presupposed a universal rather than a local value.

In Tange's work, bamboo, walkways, images of nature, and architectural stereotypes often appear as motifs that he continually reworks in his building designs, from the Tange Residence in Setagaya-ku (Tokyo, 1953) and the Kagawa Prefectural Government Office (1955 to 1958), to the Grand Écran Italie in Paris (1991), the United Overseas Bank Plaza (Singapore, 1995), and the Fuji-Sankei Communications Group Headquarters Building (Tokyo, 1996). The "ethnic" element of the language of things is subsumed in a universal principle that resolves oppositions and contrasts. The words of Yanagi Sōetsu are useful in a discussion of Japan and its style in relation to the ancient and the modern, or tradition and the avant-garde. Every artistic movement attempts to renew itself, but the true essence of beauty can manifest itself only if the distinction between old and new is erased. This idea is especially applicable to the work of Tange, who, in his modernist and functionalist stance, is inspired by two fundamental elements of Japanese tradition, which he adapts and transforms: nature and harmony. Nature is perceived through a Shinto and Buddhist lens and translated into a sensibility that does not emphasize the creative "I" (namely, the protagonist or "starchitect") but instead allows the forms to appear, essentially, as an expression of the spirit of nature. At this point, it is appropriate to complement this theme with that of the void, which is never a negation or an *a priori* condition, but the manifestation of an *originary* cosmic setting. In this sense, in Tange's work, not only do the ancient and the modern meet, but so too do the East and the West, whereby rationalism and "irrationalism" are reconciled. Sensibility, then, is an aura, but it is also loving care for the object being created. In this poetic process, artisanship and art converge in the "doing (things) well," in terms of the quality of the aesthetic life and the appropriateness of choice. Nature and the work of human beings resonate with each other. It is important to stress that nature is the common principle in all art of the Far East. Its essence is the way of illumination, which we recognize in the form and sound of bamboo, the light on peach blossoms, and the lessons of the wind passing through the trees. It is the way of *satori*, which had such an effect on the mind of André Malraux; truth and reality, illusion and imagination cancel each other out. The vastness of the rivers and mountains can be evoked with only a few instruments, and infinite occasions of pleasure created in an instant. Japanese culture is exemplary in this sense.

I feel the need to stress the symbolic value of the walkway, which connects the external and internal gaze. It is like walking on a wooden carpet in a void. Strolling in an area entirely dedicated to nature signals the dissolution of the "I" in the display of elements. It is a form of adoration *in fieri* that grows as we observe the cliff, the tree and its roots, the moss, and the drop of water; we feel the humidity in the air and hear the sound of the water of the sea, the lake, and the rivulet, and we see the fire in the brazier, and the shimmering lights on the hill. The walkway invites us to experience this spiritual state. In his essential design, Tange merges the internal and external gaze to suggest an historical memory without expressing directly the spiritual aspect of Japanese tradition, which inspires and is implied in his design. The linear and vertical elements, and the series of covered walkways forming a progression of vistas of the surrounding environment, interrupted by the supporting poles, evoke purity and eternity, doing so through their simplicity rather than the richness of their materials, which are suited to the dignity of remembrance and its ethical and sacred value.

We can now return to Europe and ask ourselves what a plausible image of the city might be. Taking into account the history of iconography, how do we imagine the city? Let us consider at least one example. During the Renaissance, Sebastiano Serlio not only identified the two types of city that provide the scenic backdrop for comedy and tragedy as appropriate theatrical vehicles with which to represent the world, he also identified in their symbolism the universal values of real cities, which contain both comedy and tragedy. On the one hand, daily life consists of events that unfold and can be portrayed in tight spaces enclosed by courtyards and architectural recesses between windows and small squares, in a web of stories that narrate ordinary lives. On the other hand are walls that converge on a central point where the drama intensifies as strong characters and a monumental atmosphere appear on the scene, where they meet, not to chat but to scream: joy and mischief on one side, pain and suffering on the other. These are the two cities – two scenarios from the world of humanity portrayed symbolically: the spirit of the marketplace and the spirit of the *agora*.

THE DEBATE BETWEEN CONSERVATIVES
AND POSTMODERNISTS

A tour of the world's megacities presents frenzy and destruction as well as the erasure of local cultures, some of which are the victims of a voracious tourism that denatures the environment. We are witnessing a true consumption of the city, that is, its human, historical, and symbolic meaning. Large electrical, telecommunications, and digital companies control vast areas of energy and transportation. The architectural styles are hybrid and eclectic, and suited to this system of civil aggregation. This is true of almost all places on earth.

In the preceding section, we examined the stereotype as a resilient model of types of created objects, a repeated and repeatable image of a manufacturing process, and a standardized model of virtuality; in other words, stereotyping gives form to things within a system of objects reproduced serially. The centuries-old synthesis of artisanship and material has been transformed in our times into design. To reconstruct an object means to retrace the techniques that produced it, including traditional ones. In terms of the relationship among technologies, there is a heated debate between those who want to defend the traces of the past as a memory important for the future, as well as a device for harmonizing the masses, and those who favour the absolute novelty of the hybrid style that is now in vogue after the modernist phase. The latter support deregulating the manufacture of architectural objects and the incoherent, improvised organization of the suburban environment. Throughout history there have been important differences of opinion on the value of humankind, quality of life, ways of thinking, and forms of culture and art. Those that exist between conservatives and postmodernists are the latest of these. We might think that, by returning to the decorative and rejecting the functional, postmodernists are promoting the recurrence of tradition, but this is not the case. In architecture, they seek the ludic element rather than the universal forms of design, which is what conservatives seek.

It all stems from the question of technologies, even though in the final analysis, technologies do not determine the primary value of architecture. As Marco Romano (2008, 108) tells us, the city is constituted not so much by a system of functions as by a system of forms, which are not merely the stones but the abstract design that incorporates the forms in the building principles:

> Only beauty satisfies these demands of the spirit because for centuries art has had the ambition of defying time – *exegi monumentum aere perennius* (I have made a monument more lasting than bronze), Horace said, and the order of beauty is instilled in humans by God himself in his likeness, according to St Augustine – and the walls of the *urbs*, the city as work of art, were invented for the purpose of offering a vision of eternity in which we can ground our earthly hopes because it is a response to a timeless invitation to identify ourselves with the *urbs* as citizens of the *civitas*, the condition of being recognized as social people. (Ibid., 109, translation by Corrado Federici)

In light of this quotation from Horace (from section three of his *Odes*), we can only agree with Romano in advocating an aesthetics that recognizes what once represented, and could continue to represent, the dignity and beauty of the city. This is not a superficial aesthetics, and as I have said earlier, it is constitutive of civilization and the destiny of its ethics.

Technology began when people first used their fingers as pliers and stones as projectiles. Like art, technology is based on the use we make of our bodies. As Mumford (1966, 19) explains, however, unlike technology, art is essentially "control over the person," and the purpose of art is to expand personality so that the feelings, emotions, attitudes, and values that manifest in a person, or in a given culture, can be transmitted along with their full meaning to other people and other cultures. In the face of the enormous power of technology and its abuses, Mumford advises that we restore our lost equilibrium by reactivating the inner and subjective element, a genuine therapy for the present and the future.

We acknowledge the importance of space by celebrating in the ritual of traveling on walkways between emptiness and fullness. We can experience this in the Katsura Imperial Villa, where the ancient tradition is echoed through the style of the famous Shinto shrine on Itsukushima, also known as Miyajima, a temple built over the water at a sacred island, considered one of the sublime landscapes of Japan. So, too, are Amanohashidate, a narrow strip of sand four kilometres long and covered with pine trees that is often evoked by writers (according to mythology it is the place where the gods created the islands of Japan), and Matsushima, a bay dotted with hundreds of small islands. Together, these are three views that all Japanese people should recognize. Miyajima is only a few kilometres from Hiroshima, which can be reached symbolically by a *torii* (gate) on the water. Itsukushima is its famous shrine. The shrine, erected in the year 593 on piles of stone in a small bay, should be visited during high tide when the structure is reflected in the water. Around it rise a pagoda with five architectural orders and various pavilions, built eight or nine centuries later. The *torii*, which seems to float on the water, makes a striking impression. When seen at twilight, when the sea, the mountain, and the shrine are tinged in various gradations of pink, the site evokes feelings described by the great poets. What is relevant to our discussion here is not the metaphysical experience but the sense of space connoted by the Japanese word *ma* (gap), understood to mean "between," that is, a duration between events, a space between objects, a relationship between two people or two different moments. It evokes the rhythm of cosmic existence that flows in the natural world and the human spirit. It implies suspending our attention, meditating on the interval between the action of the actor and the image frozen in time. *Ma* captures the moment in which the duality of action and the mind is eliminated. It is connected to incompleteness, asymmetry, and imperfection; at the same time, it affirms the calmness of contemplation. It looks at distance itself, suspending reason and feeling, and at the same time celebrates the intermediate state between emptiness and fullness. It also pertains to the spirituality created when we are in a small room in a traditional house with a window looking out on a garden (*shoin*). This is a spiritual and aesthetic dimension similar to a *wabi-sabi* (acceptance of transience) worldview, which involves both the interior and the exterior, as in a correspondence between subjectivity and objectivity, or something ungraspable. It can be called an affective state of contemplation.

These references to Japan are important because the aesthetic-artistic issue is not raised in Japanese culture in terms of either/or. Returning to the West, what sort of balanced relationship could exist between technology and beauty so as to enable architecture and the city, in the form they occupy together in space, to express autonomy and heteronomy. This is discussed above in reference to Tange, Adorno, Cacciari, Romano, and Mumford. There are those who speak of the end of the city and those who reject the idea of the end of architecture. In his comments on the city, Leonardo Benevolo (2011, 6) refers to urban sprawl (a secure setting visible from medium and short distances) and the representation of an enigmatic monumental nature: a group of buildings distinguished by what surrounds them. The fact is that cities today are indistinguishable from the territory around them. As a result, the city almost no longer exists in the historic sense. Vittorio Gregotti (2008, 21, 61), however, asserts that the task of the architect is to express thought as form. It is a question of poetics: the objects of the architect are his theory. With its concrete objects, architecture offers not only a perspective on reality but, above all, the motives and the need to reconfigure that reality. In the process of becoming the work and in the intentionality it conveys, theory is the constituent material of architecture inasmuch as it is art: a dialogue between subject and object, between presentation and representation that displays the complexity of relationships. It is, therefore, the *poiesis* produced by a specific *techne*, giving rise to a variety of ways of acting in the city and interpreting it.

In the context of disquieting transitions, throughout which the value of metaphor and symbol is in decline, it seems worthwhile to compare two different architects: one more respectful of form and harmony, the other more bizarre and nonconformist. The first is closer to the conservative spirit and the other to deconstruction. They are David Chipperfield and Frank Gehry.

In the works of Chipperfield, we sense a modernist disposition that is not merely and exclusively functionalist. He adopts the non-extremist elements of this movement, especially that of the creative genius Mies van der Rohe. He rejects the so-called "international style," seen everywhere, and believes that architecture is an encounter and a gift. Chipperfield explores in concrete ways the relationship with what already exists in the places around the world where his projects are installed. He emphasizes simplicity, congruity, lightness, and harmony in buildings, lines, surfaces, and colours using detailed segments and effects. How we feel and see depends on the size of the object and our angle of observation. His works convey a "natural" relationship with the surrounding landscape. To enter, linger, and move about in the Neues Museum in Berlin is to be embraced by the ideas that the architect transmits by joining the original and the new. We sense that the city is alive in the mind of the artist who translates it and communicates through it the communal (as opposed to solipsistic) spirit of architecture for the sake of finding a soul, that is to say, a common, inspirational, profound, intangible principle and awareness.

Among Gehry's works, I would like to comment on one of his most recent: the Louis Vuitton Foundation museum in Paris, inaugurated in October 2014, a structure that inspires awe. This time, instead of a shocking contrast with pre-existing architecture, the city of Paris displayed an architectural object in a park: the Bois de Boulogne. Gehry's Vuitton building changes depending on one's point of view; delicacy and flexibility are constants, creating a pleasant ambiguity that changes as we move about. Next to the museum are gigantic eggshells arranged on a large lawn, some haphazardly on their sides and others upright. Elsewhere is a spaceship, and an enormous dying butterfly. Changing our point of observation reveals an amorphous cloud with long, white shafts projecting from its lining, reminiscent of goose feathers. Inside, the walls look like sails billowing in the wind, though firmly held in place by a white, pure, multifaceted structure. All this is a vision or transparency, with the interior and exterior engaged in a permanent dialogue – the glass and Plexiglas partitions immerse us in the surrounding nature, in the woods and fields, while from a large terrace high above, we can enjoy a 360-degree view of the city in the distance. It is a mechanical bird, the product of a surprising architectural imagination – the museum invites us to gaze and to discover as we venture along split-levels. The architectural form appears to sail and soar while remaining static, in response to our emotions and movements. Like an enormous chrysalis or a drifting iceberg, it constantly changes and excites us. The architecture seems to display itself as it disappears and reappears with the changing light, causing the entire structure to be reflected in a small lake and its cascade.

These are two architects and two visions of the world. In one we have inspired order, and in the other, a neo-baroque form of deconstruction. Aesthetic truth and the truth of beauty have many facets. The one implies the other. We find here an ancient dilemma. In these objects, we find signs of the imitation of nature; but is nature being studied like a universe of forms or a patrimony of symbols that refer to a substance? As Roman Ingarden reminds us, architecture is the most creatively constructive of all the human arts; it embodies new forms, which is to say new creative images and correspondences. It is a product of human cohabitation with materials. It leaves its imprint on surfaces, and derives from them a spiritual and emotional model: a process rich in inner pleasure.

The debate between postmodernists and conservatives is complex, taking on a different twist at different points in time, and concerning not just architects but artists and writers as well. It also includes differences between postmodernists and deconstructionists. In addition to the well-known features, there are works difficult to define that reflect the influence of post-structuralism, such as those of Farshid Moussavi, a British-Iranian. For example, her undulating residential tower in Montpellier (2013), which exhibits a functional style and evokes ideas from her books on ornament and form. It is also reminiscent of a slightly earlier project, the Residhome Nanterre La Défense residence. The concept allows for the play of split-levels in relation to that which surrounds the building. In her work and writing, she stresses the active, rather than the symbolic, notion of ornament, which she sees as a social structure in the context of current changes with people and technology. She also stresses an approach to form and function that privileges architecture not only as product that is executed with a sense of finality, but also as a whole that integrates different elements, subjects, colours, and materials. Intermediate cases, such as this, which fall outside debates on art, are many.

Renzo Piano is a different case altogether. Apart from his thoughts pertaining to the great responsibility of the architect, both aesthetically and ethically, is another useful thought of his, in celebration of slowness, found in his writings on his own work:

> The condition for creating is made up of many contradictory states of mind. It is made up of serenity and tension, calm and energy, slowness and speed. I am slow in my approach; I am not one who takes off like a shot. I allow things to settle. However, in slowness there is great speed, great agility of mind. In the reflections of someone who writes and reasons slowly, there are a thousand connections that occur in hundredths of a second. It is a speed that no computer can match … Technology has a minimal impact on the substance of our thinking. (Piano 2010, 47, translation by Corrado Federici)

Some cities were born recently and are the product of precise planning or decision making. This applies to Brasília – planned by Lúcio Costa, with architect Oscar Niemeyer in charge of the major building, and landscape designer Roberto Burle Marx – which was inspired by a Le Corbusier design. This also applies to other great cities born in the early years of the 1700s and built according to a completely invented plan, such as Saint Petersburg. Citing the founding of a city that is not ancient allows me to make observations from a different point of view than that of architects and their aesthetic movements, namely, that of the material city. I would like to discuss Saint Petersburg, a rational eighteenth-century Enlightenment city, with its regular plan, located on the border between Estonia and Finland. It was founded by Peter the Great in 1703 as a fortress to defend against Swedish incursions. Architects and artists from Italy's Ticino region and other European countries worked on the project. It was the capital of Russia for about two centuries and enjoyed periods of glory during the 1700s and 1800s. Austere with its neoclassical and baroque buildings, it can be considered an extraordinary work and the cultural gateway to Russia. Here, reminders of recent antiquity and vestiges of the modern meet. The dispute between traditionalists and modernists dies as the city comes into view. Angelo Maria Ripellino has the following to say about this structure:

> An architectural marvel erected on unstable swampland, Petersburg appears in the pages of Russian writers as an absurd city of enchantment. Behind magnificent exteriors, austere palaces, lacy balustrades, the "Palmyra of the North," which rose like a mirage from the marsh mud through the stubborn will of a despot, hides wretched, suffering ruins, a plaintive world of sorrow. (1961, v, translation by Corrado Federici)

THE DECLINE OF THE CITY

We have already discussed the city and its origins, but it is important to recall this theme now as I am about to talk about its inexorable decline, in order to understand the reasons for this decline. In discussing the city and the sites of its establishment, Hippocrates (*On Airs, Waters and Places*) argued that the best place for a community to settle would be an ideal position (on a hilltop) with access to a coastline and the hinterland. In essence, the location must meet four conditions: have a healthy environment, be a good position for defense and the conduct of war (with available water), be a favourable location for political activity, and be surrounded by a beautiful land (as noted earlier). The essence of the city, however, resides in a different feature, which the four conditions imply and whose importance persists through the centuries – that is, the sense of community, law, and state. As Aristotle writes:

> Therefore, everyone naturally has the impulse for such a
> [political] community, but the person who first established
> [it] is the cause of very great benefits. For man, when per-
> fected, is the best of animals, but, when separated from law
> and justice, he is the worst of all; since armed injustice is
> the more dangerous, and he is equipped at birth with arms,
> meant to be used by intelligence and virtue, which he may
> use for the worst ends. Wherefore, if he have not virtue,
> he is the most unholy and the most savage of animals.
> (1943, 1, 7)

Basically, I want to underscore the idea of community and the value of virtue because they define the formation of the city; people come together and identify with their laws. In addition to these fundamental principles, is one – more descriptive but also fundamental – that has to do with forms, that is, the ancient apotropaic symbolism of the labyrinth and the enigma, which suggests protecting the mysteriousness of the community in its encounter with foreigners, as Rykwert (2008, 167–73) has noted.

These values of affirming and protecting in accordance with a desire for order and improvement have disappeared. Since the end of the 1900s, we find ourselves in a phase in which the city is in decline, in terms of its identity and allure. It is a slow process deriving from its transformation into a metropolis in the mid-1800s, which can be interpreted in terms of the philosophy of money, the labour market, and the sociology of the senses. The evolution of capitalism and post-capitalism offers mobility and speed in a universe of perceptions characterized increasingly by anxiety and fear. As Simmel observed in the early part of the last century, the metropolitan landscape induces profound changes in the very forms of sensibility and consciousness as humanity becomes indifferent, disillusioned, and sated. A sort of *blasé* attitude makes everything appear grey and uniform. In reaction to this is the dizzying emergence of the eccentric, which gives rise to pathologies of excitement, and at the same time an anaesthesia in fashion, media, and the arts. The centuries-old aesthetic distance between object and subject is swept away by trends in participation or passivity. Films and the avant-gardes dish out visual and psychological shock. A constellation of images, from Futurism to Dziga Vertov, illustrate Simmel's argument, which he developed from Benjamin. In their writings, Nietzsche and Spengler reflect on the eclipse of the city and portray the decadence of a culture and a world. Nietzsche articulates two interesting positions in *Thus Spoke Zarathustra* (1883) and *Human, All Too Human* (1878). Upon his return from the Isles of the Blessed, Zarathustra decides to mingle once more with humans in order to avoid the solipsistic visions that would lead him far from the lifestyle of his day. He wants to know what has happened to humanity during his absence: whether it has become greater or smaller. The great city is the first place he encounters where he can carry out his research. In front of a row of new houses, he says with surprise:

> What do these houses mean? Verily, no great soul put them up as its simile! Did perhaps a silly child take them out of its toy-box? Would that another child put them again into the box!
>
> And these rooms and chambers – can men go out and in there? They seem to be made for silk dolls; or for dainty-eaters, who perhaps let others eat with them. (2010, Part 3, 5)

Nietzsche provides the answer in the section titled "On Virtue That Makes Small." Zarathustra stops and, troubled, says: "There hath everything become smaller," pointing out how only small people can enter such dwellings. This limitation symbolizes the rage of the modern, narrow-minded people who cannot forgive Zarathustra for failing to envy their virtues, which are themselves becoming increasingly small. Their entire world is now reduced to a very modest size. This is so demoralizing for Nietzsche's protagonist that he says, "it is hard for me to understand that small people are necessary." In the city of his times, people have become smaller and smaller, which accounts for their doctrine of happiness and comfort. In fact, people have such moderate virtues because they want comfort. But a moderate virtue is compatible only with comfort, and an equally silly happiness is only compatible with small-mindedness. In the great city, Zarathustra meets "the ape," which imitates him and tells him that he has nothing to find and only something to lose in the city, and advises him to go back. Zarathustra, however, tells him to be quiet, and concludes his discourse on the great city with the following words:

> I loathe also this great city, and not only this fool. Here and there – there is nothing to better, nothing to worsen.
>
> Woe to this great city! – And I would that I already saw the pillar of fire in which it will be consumed! For such pillars of fire must precede the great noontide. But this has its time and its own fate. –
>
> This precept, however, give I to you, in parting, you fool: Where one can no longer love, there should one – pass by! –
>
> Thus spoke Zarathustra, and passed by the fool and the great city. (2010, Part 3, 7)

This apocalyptic image, which foreshadows the future devastation of the 1900s, captures a widespread decadence (the hypocrisy and falseness of a small-minded humanity and its projects), as we have noted previously. This is a vision of the destiny of the city, beyond any moral or aesthetic criteria, without nostalgia or utopian ideals. Nietzsche, however, offers this interpretation of the metropolis as he describes the cultural situation at the end of the nineteenth century, because the city itself seems to embody destiny. In the passages in *Human, All Too Human* in which he comments on the "age of comparison," Nietzsche emphasizes the abandonment of tradition, the fermentation of emotions, the restlessness of people, and "the polyphony of strivings." He equates all of this with a proliferation of artistic stages and genres that are copied simultaneously, as are the stages and genres of morality, custom, and civilization. This is the age of the feverish metropolis about which Simmel was to write a few years later:

> Such an age acquires its significance through the fact that in it the various different philosophies of life, customs, cultures can be compared and experienced side by side; which in earlier ages, when, just as all artistic genres were attached to a particular place and time, so every culture still enjoyed only a localized domination, was not possible. Now an enhanced aesthetic sensibility will come to a definitive decision between all these forms offering themselves for comparison: most of them – namely all those rejected by this sensibility – it will allow to die out. There is likewise now taking place a selecting out among the forms and customs of higher morality whose objective can only be the elimination of the lower moralities. This is the age of comparison! (Nietzsche 1986, 23)

Nietzsche goes on to say that the correlation between the increase in aesthetic feeling and ethical habits is the source of both pride and suffering in this age. But this is our task, and posterity will bless us, says the philosopher, because generations will succeed us that will be beyond cultures that are now finished, as well as beyond the culture of comparison, in that they will be able to look back and see both the original culture and the culture of comparison as "venerable antiquities." In this text, we find different reflections and inflections relating to *Thus*

Spoke Zarathustra. Nietzsche understands the great variety of elements that make up the city at the root of western civilization, in which the new and the traditional are celebrated. The beginning of an historic redemption of humanity seems evident in these comments. The metropolis, which has within it the movement of uprooted people, as well as a profound change of direction for human habitation outside the *polis*, the Medieval, Renaissance, and baroque city of the marketplace, draws humanity away from a destiny of decline and onto a different path.

In discussing the decline of a culture (*kultur*), focusing on its final stage – defined as "civilization" (*zivilisation*) – it seems opportune to cite Oswald Spengler, who interprets this vision. He says that we are declining and that we see our decline as it unfolds. We see ourselves at an end while superior cultures become civilizations.

> Today, at the end of this same culture, a vague spirituality without roots flows through every possible species of landscape and intellectual horizon. The intermediate period was that in which humans knew how to die for a piece of land. The intermediate period of this city is tied to the peasant culture and its history has come to an end.
> (Spengler 1981, 777)

Furthermore, this phenomenon is seen on various continents throughout the history of cultures. The history of the city has a conclusion: from the marketplace of its origins, it becomes the city of civilization and ends as a cosmopolis. Everywhere on earth, human labour, expressed in the nobility of living and building, is being sacrificed to this evolution, whose ultimate fruit is the spirit of civilization, in other words, the self-destruction of the constituent values of culture. "Race suicide" is connected to this idea, with decreasing birth rates serving as a powerful sign of decline and the end. This is the view of Spengler, who devotes many pages to the crisis of societies and their decline as he compares cultures over the long course of their self-destruction. In civilizations, we find abandoned provincial towns, and at the end of the cycle, giant deserted cities consisting of piles of rubble, among which sparse populations live in extremely stark conditions, as people did in prehistoric times. The author dwells on vast, abandoned urban landscapes overgrown with weeds with the passage of time. In the fifth century, Rome had the population of a village; Pataliputra, the residence of Ashoka, was a deserted wasteland, as the Chinese traveller Xuanzang described it in 635; Sumatra was abandoned in the tenth century; and the great Mayan cities must have already been deserted during the days of Hernán Cortés. Let us go further back in time. Between 220 and 146 BCE, Polybius described many famous cities, either deserted or in ruins, and told of *fora* and *gymnasia* where animals grazed, or amphitheatres whose importance could be gleaned from surviving statues and busts found where grain now grew. Entire cultures have been swallowed up from within in a process of "internal extinction." According to Spengler, we encounter the same phenomenon, and for the same reasons, in the Alexandrian and Roman societies, as well as in every society that became a civilization, including the one in which Buddhism developed, Hellenism, and the twentieth century, no less than in the days of Laozi or the doctrine of Charvaka. In all civilizations, a multi-century process of depopulation begins: "the whole pyramid of cultural man vanishes" (Spengler 1981, 105). The disintegration starts at the apex, then extends to the metropolises, reaches the provincial towns, and affects the countryside, which, with the best people leaving in increasing numbers, delays for a period of time the depopulation of the city.

We can see this process in the dying peasant culture, according to this reconstruction of the history of humankind: intelligence and thought are replaced by an unconscious experience of life that is thereby weakened, and scientific theory takes the place of religious myth. As has already happened at the start of the 1900s, we are witnessing "the sterility of civilized man" (ibid., 102). This cannot be explained by the laws of causality, which is to say, science:

It is to be understood as an essentially *metaphysical* turn towards death. The last man of the world-city no longer *wants* to live – he may cling to life as an individual, but as a type, as an aggregate, no, for it is a characteristic of this collective existence that it eliminates the terror of death. That which strikes the true peasant with a deep and inexplicable fear, the notion that the family and the name may be extinguished, has now lost its meaning. The continuance of the blood-relation in the visible world is no longer a duty of the blood, and the destiny of being the last of the line is no longer felt as a doom. (Spengler 1981, 103–4)

The home and property, which are the basis of the principle of the city, the trench in the ground, as has been mentioned several times, are not the elusive connection between the body and goods, but a lasting and internal union of *eternal* land and *eternal* blood. In this interpretation, only by means of a mystical form of sedentariness do the great stages of life (procreation, birth, and death) acquire a metaphysical aura that is condensed symbolically in the customs and religion of all non-nomadic peoples of the countryside. For the last humans of civilization, however, all this no longer exists.

In the modern cosmopolises, which we encounter at the end of the cycle of every great culture, intellectual tensions tend toward a single, specific, urban form of recreation: relaxation and "distraction." These are terms that Benjamin describes in his analysis, which opens up new possibilities. Here instead, play, the pleasure of living, and euphoria are associated with a cosmic rhythm and are seen, therefore, as not being understood by modernity, which, together with the myth of daily work, promotes a spasmodic attention to gambling, sports, and sensual or emotional tension. As the author tells us, cinema, expressionism, theosophy, boxing, dancing, poker, and betting on horses can all be found in a different form in ancient Rome. As well, analogous phenomena can be found in China, India, and the Arabian Peninsula. On the basis of these distractions from the *taedium vitae* engaged in by metropolitan men and women, in whose mind there is no longer any trace of the countryside, a form of religion still exists, but in the sense of a pleasure that is the same and found everywhere across the ages.

In its imperial splendour, Rome and Baghdad, Babylon and Tenochtitlan in their moment of glory but on the verge of decline were like the London or Berlin of today following the First World War. We cannot grasp "the madness of this development [where no compulsion] avails to neutralize the attractive force of these demonic creations" (ibid., 102). But the fact is that we are heading toward the end: the peasant home and the buildings of the city relate to each other the way spirit and intelligence and blood and stone do, according to Spengler. Only the body remains of the formal ideal of the person of antiquity. The giant cities of the present era extend to infinity with their suburbs and communications networks, whereas ancient metropolises strove only to become more compact. From organic growth, we have passed to an inorganic piling up of structures, beyond the typical horizon of the cities of urban architects. Our relationship with the land has come to an end and the society of money has imposed itself like a despot. The soul of the city both old and new has a face and a language, a universe of forms and habits. The soul narrates and shows. The link with the land has been broken. "The immemorially old roots of Being are dried up in the stone-masses of its cities. And the free intellect – fateful word! – appears like a flame, mounts splendid into the air, and pitiably dies" (ibid., 92).

This description is definitely interesting, but it does not address the complexity of the world we face. When reading this section of *The Decline of the West*, where the city is described as a pile of ruins and desolation, I have the impression of being in Marcantonio Raimondi's "Dream of Raphael," or a painting by Hieronymus Bosch, a work by Monsù Desiderio, John Martin's famous illustrations for John Milton's Pandæmonium, or the world of H.P. Lovecraft. There are also images such as those we might find in a science fiction film. As Spengler states:

The city is intellect. The Megalopolis is "free" intellect. It is
in resistance to the "feudal" powers of blood and tradition
that the burgherdom or bourgeoisie, the intellectual class,
begins to be conscious of its own separate existence. It
upsets thrones and limits old rights in the name of reason
and above all in the name of … the People, which hencefor-
ward means exclusively the people of the city. Democracy is
the political form in which the townsman's outlook upon
the world is demanded of the peasantry also. The urban
intellect reforms the great religion of the springtime and
sets up by the side of the old religion of noble and priest,
the new religion of the Tiers État, *liberal science.* The city
assumes the lead and control of economic history in replac-
ing the primitive values of the land, which are forever inseparable from the life and thought of the rustic, by the
absolute idea of money as distinct from goods. (Ibid., 96–7)

The birth of the *soul* of a city, therefore, is "the miracle" of
human history that comes to life in a visible body. From a group
of dwellings, a corner of a picturesque village, emerges a living
whole that grows, acquires form in a vast array of styles, and
injects a language into the natural and the cultivated land. What
is natural becomes artificial.

It is undeniable that we would agree with Spengler's notion
of the catastrophic collapse of peasant culture, and to a certain
extent his reconstruction of the history of the city; however,
many criticisms from an historical, sociological, and anthropological point of view can be levelled against this text, interesting
as it is. The cultures of the world in the early part of the third
millennium are clearly not headed for depopulation, and cities
are not deserted; rather, they have been transformed into enormous urban landscapes. Spengler wrote *The Decline of the West*
in 1918, immediately after the First World War. We need to mit-
igate and compensate for the more exuberant aspects of his
writing as well as for the excessively imaginative interpretation
of world history contained in the chapter on the city written by
Max Weber in 1920 in his *Economy and Society,* a book that

appeared posthumously in 1922. From Weber, we learn that the city is the highest symbol of free social rationality, which is a feature of the West. In short, the industrial metropolis is an economic space, a place for consumerism, production, and commerce. The "ideal type" of city created over the course of history through the free association of people as a response to tyranny, absolutism, and barbarism, has proven to be a force that harmonizes the artisanal-industrial centre and the countryside, autonomy and centralization, and direct representation of citizens and the institutions representing more complex units, such as states and nations. As Enzo Paci (2007, 34, translated by Corrado Federici) asserts, "To study the sociology of the city was, for Weber, and remains so in part for us, to search in history for the signs of our destiny."

LOSS OF THE CENTRE

We have spoken about large cities, Braudel's world-cities, the relationship between city and state, the world economy in the age of globalization, and the cultural crisis in the modern metropolis. In his *Spettri di Marx* (*Spectres of Marx*), in which he analyzes the phenomena of deconstruction, Derrida defines *ontopology* as the union of ontological value, which relates to citizenship and the sense of belonging, and the establishment of a permanent locality, with the aim of producing a new identity for the community, including public and private space, while a discussion of politics is deferred. The emptiness of the ontological response has created a separation or disconnect between things and words, and between actions and consciousness.

However, these considerations on where we find ourselves and on the group to which we belong shape our impressions, including our daily impressions of ordinary life, and affect the way we see and feel. The sense of fragmentation created a century ago with the onset of modernism in our social and interior lives through technology, innovations, and the shock of representation (and the imagination), has extended into the postmodern, that is, today's world of media communications.

What, then, separates (or distinguishes) what is central from what is peripheral in the evolution of urban space? I have in mind the city from the Middle Ages to the 1700s, where Rococo combines with the principles of the Enlightenment. A process of great disfigurement and decentralization begins in the 1800s. Through the gaze, the aesthetic approach to the idea and the dream of dwelling is integrated with an anthropological and cultural approach. In contemporary architecture, building stereotypes are commonplace, and *kitsch* prevails: it seems that the idea and the dream of dwelling without losing sight of its symbols have been lost. We could say that *comfort* has impoverished the deep, psychological meaning associated with the home for centuries, changing it into something inauthentic. The home, however, is not the objective of human activity but a sort of condition in which it can take place – its experiential refuge, according to Emmanuel Lévinas. Thanks to this affective state, people are not thrown brutally into the world and abandoned. Simultaneously within and without, they go into the external world from the sweetness of their inwardness. The dwelling can be seen as a "custom" among many "customs," but it is in the system of finalities that the home occupies a special position. We live between the inner world and the outer world, between the of subject and the world, as Lévinas states:

> The recollection necessary for nature to be able to be represented and worked over, for it to first take form as a world, is accomplished as the home. Man abides in the world as having come to it from a private domain, from being at home with himself, to which at each moment he can retire. He does come to it from an intersidereal space where he would already be in possession of himself and from which at each moment he would have to recommence a perilous landing … The intimacy which is familiarity already presupposes is an *intimacy with someone*. The interiority of recollection is a solitude in a world already human. Recollection refers to a welcome. (1979, 152–5)

Let us now examine the dwelling in the context of the urban reality. Even if we do not examine the genesis of creative *deregulation* in the postmodern era, as Philip Johnson does, we can still cite one of Johnson's statements from the end of the 1970s to comment on a situation that has frequently been underscored: "It is evident that our cities decline for the same reasons our air is being polluted. We do not worry enough about it because our values do not have beauty as their end. Two values stand out … money and utility" (1985, 124). Nearly fifty years have passed, but the situation has not changed significantly. Europe, which seemed to resist economic imperatives more than other continents, is sliding into this cultural abyss. London is an example, as are the new standards for preserving historic centres in Italy, France, and other parts of Europe.

At more or less the same time, Hans Sedlmayr described a sense of epochal disorientation of our sensibilities, associated with the end of intuition and transcendance, and he spoke of the loss of light in the age of secularization. For him, the idea of art was shattered by chaos and the absence of humanity. I do not wish to restate his position or his response to post-war society and the avant-gardes. We should take the loss of the centre as a metaphor for the current situation, which seems to be one of frenzy and destruction: devastation, the erasure of memory, the obliteration of traditions. I would like, instead, to draw the reader's attention to Sedlmayr's invitation, which I summarize as follows: The wound created in this transitional era of increasingly innovative technologies raises hope for a balance between the new and the old. Sedlmayr says that we need to find a way to make Blaise Pascal's maxim effective: It is only because we do not know how to properly study and explain the present that we use our intelligence to imagine the future.

Let us, therefore, try to interpret the present by thinking of a world that is close to us and that may be better than the one we inhabit. I would like to make two observations regarding the present and the future. The first emphasizes the importance of narrativity; the second promotes a technologically intelligent city, the so-called "smart city."

Is storytelling in the new urban context still possible? In terms of our emotional response to buildings and roads, how can we safeguard a pleasurable sort of *flânerie* or a completely personal way of "mapping"? What is the sensibility that moves us as we stroll through the main city square, the cathedral, and the outskirts of the city? We sometimes find ourselves huddled together and protected in the city, as if we were in an intimate setting, but if we look into the distance, the city skyline seems unending and we feel ourselves dissolving in the vastness of the horizon. How can we escape the anguish we feel in urban spaces? Storytelling is one form of therapy. Let us seek to refine our instruments of understanding and become attuned to the world in its potential for evoking emotional states. At the same time, let us attempt to interpret the concept of space, which Foucault carefully studied some decades ago. What is the meaning of space when it is perceived both within and without any "design" it may have? I ask this because there is a difference between living within a manufactured object, such as a house designed and constructed for the modern cosmopolis, and seeing this object as part of a social style of doing and representing. To dwell aesthetically in a city means to identify the visible, structural features of the houses, public buildings, monuments, and squares. The way rooms open onto a patio or street, the vertical or horitontal axis of buildings, the grouping of buildings, and the way streets intersect comprise a dynamics based on a poetic organization of movements and glances. We are the protagonists of the *ethos*, that is, the spirit of the city, as well as of the *oikos* (family) or community to which we belong. In the distribution of buildings and materials, and in our movements through them, there is a precise relationship with the deep meaning of narration (both individual and social) that has always been an integral part of the human adventure. In fact, we can think of the city as a text made of stones, a graphic invention, a mesh of symbols and meanings with grammatical and syntactic elements that form a rhetoric of space enlivend by recurring images. We move though many labyrinths for the pleasure we get from doing so and the pleasure of looking – but with what feelings and actions? This applies to the unfinished or metallic walls of a work by Le Corbusier or Gehry as much as to vertical grassy strips on architecture. The narrative thread continues to be spun despite the changes the city undergoes, because we are responsible for making the universe of forms come alive on a daily basis: we who are the protagonists of the endless adventure that is the pursuit of knowledge.

Now we may ask ourselves if a smart city really exists. We would like it to. We are compelled to ask this question when institutions do not answer your calls, when you are waiting for a bus that never arrives, and when you ride on an uncomfortable train to go to the ourskirts of the city. Smart is the word that large electric and communications companies use when trying to come up with solutions to the drawbacks of urban development. I suspect that this is a deception because citizens do not seem to be involved. Poverty, immigration, revolt in the suburbs, and the inconveniences of travel are a political problem, not just a technical one.

It would seem that mid-sized cities with a population of less than 500,000 are able to offer a good quality of life to their inhabitants and a healthy environment, in a way that larger cities can not. But this is not necessarily so. When it comes to cities like these, Rudolf Giffinger critiques the assumed link between social development, new technologies, and quality of life, and emphasizes the importance of social, political, and cultural factors as well. The problem, however, is not the mid-sized cities of Europe but the megacities of the rest of the world.

Carlo Ratti, on the other hand, seems more interested in the technological semiosphere of "urban intelligence." In this he is not exploring the idea of the city; rather, he uses the term to refer only to a set of data – a kind of "outdoor computer," or a hybrid in which citizens are the engine for the future city. But it is inconsistent or abstract to link everything to communications systems. After identifying its requirements, the "smart city" would make the system of services simpler and more efficient for citizens, trim bureaucracy, promote organizational cooperation, improve the quality of urban services – from waste disposal and social assistance to providing green areas and improvements in education – regulate energy consumption and spending, and balance the expansion of built-up areas with natural landscapes. A situation such as this would please everyone, but it is somewhat worrying that cities that have the opposite of this sort of enlightened administration have been given the Smart City award. The "smart city" seems to be one that pursues the vision of engineers and planners, and is indifferent to the participation and activity of citizens. At its root, the "smart city" has no real democratic thought bringing together industry and political will in a positive proposal for the common good. It is elitist and presumes to have decision-making power over citizens. It does not consider that creative spontaneity can sometimes replace institutions. This is not even to speak of poverty in the megacities, the two billion living in poverty on the urbanized land of this planet – nor of critical sociology. It is true that some cities of the world adopt an intelligent system, but in many others it is just used as a pretext to attract funds. The most interesting aspects of the intelligent city, however, only function if its political administration is intelligent.

There is one undeniable and disturbing fact: everything in the world is subject to fraying. The question, then, arises with regard to architecture in light of this loss of a centre, the worrisome emptying of meaning, and the spiritual and emotional deadening of humanity.

In discussing architecture in *Truth and Method*, Hans-Georg Gadamer dwells on the term "ornament." In order to grasp the aesthetic quality of a work, we need to extrapolate from its historical, ethical, cognitive, and functional content. We need to seek out the *erlebnis*, or experience, as if from the emotional perspective of a subject standing before a work of art produced by another subject. Where can we locate the representational element of architecture when we consider this work of art as a copy of an original, and we want instead to present it as an ontological artwork? The function and location are its "representation." Even after the original function disappears, the building retains a sort of memory. What is represented is ornament, which is not a superficial detail but an element necessary to the essence of the artistic fact. The manufactured object attracts the observer, and at the same time refers to something else: the context of the life that surrounds it. As spatial constructs, architectural forms embrace painting, sculpture, poetry, music, dance, and theatre. We can conclude, then, that there is a correlation between ornament and beauty, which has been understood since antiquity. The capacity for self-representation, subject to mediation, "does not allow architecture to stand apart from its context."

> Architecture has two forms of mediation. As a spatial art, it is both art that gives form to space and art that creates space. We have not only all the ways of organizing the ornamentation of space, but in its essence it is decorative. The essence of ornamentation consists in the fact of that two-sided mediation: it attracts to itself the attention of the observer, satisfies his or her taste; on the other hand, it sends the observer beyond the self, toward the vaster vital context that accompanies it … We might say that ornamentation belongs to representation, but representation is an ontological fact; it is *repraesentatio*. An ornamental motif, a decoration, and a sculpture conspicuously on display are representations in the same sense that, let us say, the church of which it is a part is. (Gadamer 1990, 194–6, translation by Corrado Federici)

To explain further Gadamer's position on the nature of a work of architecture, consider his words on the relevance of beauty, which relate less to the beauty of ornamentation and more to the object and the image of the object. Here we have the "constructive" and unifying meaning that over the course of history has tied together the idea of the central plan and the nave. What, we may ask, is its aesthetic raison d'être?

> The reply of the church [to this question] … persuades each visitor. In a sense, the tension between the nave and the central part of the church returns it once again to a unity, but in such a way that the space changes for those who walk through it, as if it could be read in two ways. (Gadamer 1986, 144, translation by Corrado Federici)

In an essay on architecture and narrative from the mid-1990s, Paul Ricœur reflects on the act of constructing and on the "living" evocation of the constructed object. He identifies three phases of architecture: prefiguration, configuration, and refiguration, which together constitute the planning of, inhabiting of, and living in the constructed object. From the relationship between the dwelling place and its surroundings is derived the heterogeneity of the structure, its intertextuality, the discourse on architectural forms carried out by the forms themselves, and the vision of the person who dwells in the structure or uses it. There is an important inner narrative at work here, consisting of spatiality and temporality as told by both the architecture and the person who experiences it. It is an art of both self-presentation and representation that comes to life in the story told by subjects who observe and move inside architectural spaces. In refiguration, memory is activated and, in a living text, reconstructs the environment that we inhabit physically, mentally, and emotionally. Thus, architecture can be read like a world in which we pursue establishing a dialogue with life stories, as narrated by monuments and buildings. As we know, we need to safeguard the past, despite the fact that it no longer exists; this indeed is what the stones that last can do. Architecture is a textual world but it is also a lived world. We are both the mediation and the memory that emanates from the object.

In explaining refiguration, Ricœur makes reference to Freud (memory-repetition, memory-reconstruction) and to Bakhtin's notion of the "chronotope," calling this form of dwelling in space-time – between wandering and staying in one place – *itinérance*.

I would like to bring this first topic of the *text of the city* to the point in which narrated time and constructed space refer to each other; they do not allow themselves to be thought separately. This reference is ensured by the idea of the *world of the text* … The relationship between geometric space and inhabited space is mediated by the story inscribed in these places of memory. This double mediation is the condition for the possibility of an exchange between narrativity and architecture on the level of "refiguration."
(Ricœur, quoted in Rocca 2008, 249, translated by Corrado Federici)

It is interesting to emphasize that, alongside the narrative art in the postmodern era, there also exists a spontaneous or refined *narrative architecture*.

In recent years, as has been already stated, virtual technologies have created previously unimagined relationships between humans and things. Urban territories, the sites of this epochal transformation, will continue to mould enormous "material" figurations. The buildings of the cosmopolis will soon be confused with their holographic (mobile) *in vivo* reproductions, able to be perceived in a bizarre form of illumination. Even more than today, in some cases we will not be able to understand the difference between reality and appearance, with all due respect to many philosophers. We will find ourselves in the interactive sphere, between the existing object and its copy, believing we are the protagonists of exciting adventures of seeing and feeling. We are about to witness significant cognitive upheavals in the face an infinite number of icons fired into cyberspace by multinational corporations on the wave of the effect of human activity on the ecosystem. What is the effect of the "smart city" in such a scenario? The political distance between citizens and institutions produces new fictions of (simulated) participation, and new totalitarianisms will be created. In addition, since notions of taste and beauty are constructs of the mind and can be only an opportunity for the economy, museums of museums will be constructed, with holograms allowing us to reproduce a manufactured good in empty space so that it appears before us. We will encounter the luminous form of so many artworks blown up to enormous size, as new optical illusions will be created. Similarly, we will find in our homes, for private and solipsistic viewing, media stars and other ubiquitous figures. The mobile hologram will satisfy our desire to be omnipotent. True and fake structures and simulated harmonies will be the source of entertainment for the world, constituting knowledge and consciousness, and pointing toward a new aesthetics. The real city will be amalgamated with the virtual city, and we will be swept up by the enchantment of new technologies.

URBAN HABITAT IN THE AGE OF GLOBALIZATION

The great transformations of recent decades and the enormous weight of the upheaval caused in the landscape and territory have given rise to a new, complex configuration of the environment. The city has become a territorial habitat to be designed, built, used, and exploited for the common good: a previously unimagined magnitude of human capacity appears to be at hand. This is the great gamble of the first half of this century. It is not a matter of inventing just any sort of design, as some would like, or of theorizing a landscape distinct from the environment and the territory, like an island with nothing but gardens, parks, and protected green spaces. The essential point is a process of humanization that contains within it the scale of urban development. The art of "doing (things) well" is also a search for the best quality of life. It is my hope that appropriate practices will be put in place to create an atmosphere (an ambiance) of lived and living experience. Since antiquity, humankind has redesigned the forms of the nature surrounding them and created a vision and an experience of social cohesion. We can only continue along this path and, in the age of globalization, in the face of the collapse of the myth of the landscape, attempt to rebuild this path's delicate natural fabric. Perhaps the territorial habitat can become an art of the post-landscape and the post-metropolis, and create harmony in the present enormous confusion.

With the values of civilization and culture now eclipsed, represented symbolically by stones and institutions, what remains of the city? What is the aesthetic meaning of the built-up landscape (a more appropriate expression to describe the new urban areas)? It seems opportune at this point to offer statistics of this change, which may provide a ray of hope. We may think of architecture as a totality of forms, materials, and colours that can reflect its essence and its presence as an object that signifies, but we may also argue that architecture develops the structural elements of that essence. Keeping in mind these two possibilities, we come to understand the world organized by people through analogy: architecture as nature, and nature as architecture. In continually forging and shaping the world, architecture itself appears to be a synthesis of the natural elements. Earth, water, air, and fire promote the interaction between the natural landscape and the constructed landscape, not only symbolically but also concretely when used in the application of technology. In reality, the act of dwelling produces forms that are different from everything that surrounds us. In this sense, architecture can be considered to be a *"sedimento resistente"* (resilient sediment), to use Paolo Portoghesi's expression. Our collective work is affected by the drama of time in the same way as nature does, in that it ends up being a part of nature.

Nevertheless, in the best cases, what is built is the result of an understanding between people and the world around them. This understanding can be found in the work and design of many architects in a poetics of space, in other words, in a conceptualizing and shaping that seeks a balance of materials and symbols. The motivation for this does not come from a clash between conservation and innovation. The focus, instead, is on the connetion between emotions and things, and on evoking an ancient accord between human work and nature. Making and using, producing and perceiving, define an object that is linked to history and to manufactured things.

The constructed landscape can be described in a few essential points: situation, relationship, and intervention. From the planning of buildings to the restoration of historic centres, works follow an ideal design of coherence among forms, materials, colours, and structure. From this perspective, building should not lead us to mutilate or destroy the order and the visible traces of the past, but to plan for a balanced continuation of the past into the future, without altering the morphology of nature or erasing the signs of the presence of humankind. Whether constructed or natural, the landscape defines an art in whose identity architects also participate. Planning has the dual function of presenting new forms in the territory and determining the environment's capacity to receive these forms; it is based on continuity. The interpretation of time and space should not negatively affect the recovery of tradition; at the same time, it should seek to express the new requirements of social life.

The meaning of the landscape derives from interventions associated with the "making of the environment." It is not simply a matter of moving on after analyzing what we see, but of creating an organic design and offering a particular physical context. It is here, perhaps, where we find the first signs of the current trend of "process orientation." This occurs when an abandoned, unused, or badly damaged area is recovered through a comprehensive rebuilding project. The aesthetics of the urban landscape requires two additional important and correlated aspects: recognition and interpretation. This is because there can be no coherence and continuity with respect to nature and culture without determining their compatibility with the identity of a place and without translating the morphological essence of the place itself in accessible terms.

Nature is closely related to a plethora of man-made structures. Towns, villages, hamlets, mountains, and cultivated spaces are historically part of our repertoire as farmers, travellers, explorers, merchants, and pilgrims. We have an immense catalogue of images of the world gathered from documents on agricultural zones, maps, and travel diaries. To the eye, architectural forms either blend with or distinguish themselves from the features of the territory and create an order among things found in the many different places. The effects of these elements, blended together, show clearly the relationship between architecture and nature, which is part of the idea of landscape itself; indeed, the words for "landscape" in French (*paysage*) and Italian (*paesaggio*) are derived from *pagus*, or village. The mirroring of natural forms in the forms of art and architecture, and vice versa, occurs when the landscape presents itself spontaneously to our eyes, and through its form creates a genuine poetics, which is appropriated in art. I mentioned this earlier in my remarks on Gadamer and Ricœur.

At the heart of the problem of form is the model. What models does the landscape offer us? We identify them in the facts that make space come alive and that are space itself. The model implies organization on the basis of order, either in parallel with or preceding visual perception, which provides not so much stability as coherence, unity, and multiplicity. In this way, shapes, outlines, and lines create figures and arabesques of things that are either regular or irregular. Form is not a canon, but a cluster of features in transformation. It cuts across materials, sensibilities, emotions, and intuitions where we see allegories and symbols converge. I have said that both the city and the landscape adopt a language. This morphology has an aesthetic life of its own. It makes no difference whether it is the cypress, olive, almond, or oak tree, or a certain quality of the earth or rocks; at the root of enchantment and myth is the phenomenology of the elements.

From the laws of the forms of nature and from the description of materials emerges a cluster of features based on impressions or qualities of the physical density of bodies or their dematerialization. Architecture plays a central role in all this by producing objects in relation to the *ecumene*, or inhabited earth, because every place in which it intervenes necessarily possesses a real and ecological aspect that is measurable, quantifiable, and tied to the *topos*, as well as an immaterial, semantic aspect that is not measurable and qualitative, and is tied, instead, to the *chora*. As Augustin Berque states, the reciprocity between these two aspects or their dynamic union shapes the places of the inhabited earth.

I would like to make a final observation on the home and the hut. According to Gaston Bachelard, we conceptualize the dwelling on the basis of a profound experience of the home. For the French philosopher, every space that is authentically and affectively inhabited carries the ideas of the home and evokes a host of feelings that nourish our earliest dreams. They do so through a sensibility born in the house in which we lived and which has remained fixed in time or suspended in our imagination. For Bachelard, who studies the places of our intimate life, the home has primary value. This way of examining the spaces of our inner life certainly concerns the home, but not the hut. This is because architecture obeys a set of plans and calculations relating to the project, the production of which is part of that delicate, mysterious process which consists of the passage from a mental to a material order, and which is not exhausted in the simple application of a premediated structure. The hut, however, does not obey any order. It is made of heterogeneous materials, often found materials, the arrangement of which depends on their characteristics so that the hut's final form is a product of nature. Once a hut has been destroyed, it is difficult to reproduce the original; even if the same elements are used, a different shelter or new type of space would be created. It is commonly thought that we dwell in houses, but not in huts. Both, however, are archetypes. Our original dwellings were huts, as Vitruvius tells us. In the second of his *Ten Books on Architecture*, which has survived without the illustrations that originally accompanied it, Vitruvius provides a narrative that was destined to inspire many. He sees fire as the original social foundation, something that was discussed earlier in this book. Humans gathered around the fire, and as a result of these gatherings, they began to communicate. Vitruvius goes on to write that fire gave us the opportunity to assemble as a society and to dwell in the same place. In this way, each individual uses his or her skills, and at the same time allows others to benefit from them: some build huts with leaves, while others dig caves in the mountains; others imitate the industriousness of the swallows that build shelters using small branches and earth – and each observes and considers the work of his or her neighbour while perfecting his or her own inventions. Each day, progress is made in the way we build, because our nature, which is docile and inclined to imitation, compels us to tell each other what we have made. In this way, primitive, rustic architecture has looked to formations occurring in nature as models: holes in the mountains that provide protection as though a lair, or structures made of branches, similar to swallow nests.

Tim Ingold (2001, 137, 138) establishes a parallel between the habitat of animals or birds and the house as a living organism. He invites us to reflect on the tree, such as an oak in which owls, squirrels, wolves, or ants live. Different factors create the conditions under which the tree assumes different forms and proportions, depending on its inhabitants. Apparently there is only a relative difference between the tree and the house. Heidegger expresses a different viewpoint in his well-known text "Building, Dwelling, Thinking." He illustrates how dwelling and building are one and the same. Humankind creates room for itself, and for this reason we are able to build. By the same token, through building we create a place that provides room:

The essence of building is letting dwell. Building accomplishes its essential process in the raising of locales by the joining of their spaces. *Only if we are capable of dwelling*, can we build. Let us think for a while of a farmhouse in the Black Forest, which was built some two hundred years ago by the dwelling of peasants. Here the self-sufficiency of the power to let sky and divinities, earth and mortals enter *in simple oneness* into things ordered the house … Building and thinking are, each in its own way, inescapable for dwelling. The two, however, are insufficient for dwelling so long as each busies itself with its own affairs in separation, instead of listening to the other. They are able to listen if both – building and thinking – belong to dwelling, if they remain within their limits and realize that the one as much as the other comes from the workshop of long experience and incessant practice. (1993, 362)

What allows a place to exist is, indeed, the capacity to build. The relationship is as follows: dwelling is the capacity for making room, and making room is the condition for building, that is, for creating a place that exists in itself. The place, therefore, makes possible the distance within its own boundaries. The hut in Ingold's comments entails a relationship involving placement in a location and building. In addition, we settle and stay in the hut and do not merely pause there. Building a hut is like making a nest; it is a process, however, that continues for the entire time in which a site is inhabited. The thought of building is contained in the very act of *dwelling*.

Bibliography

Abruzzese, Alberto, and Aldo Bonomi, eds. 2004. *La città infinita* (The endless city). Milan: Bruno Mondadori.

Abu-Lughod, Janet. 1999. *New York, Chicago, Los Angeles: America's Global Cities*. Minneapolis: University of Minnesota Press.

Adorno, Theodor W. 1975. *Teoria estetica*, ed. Enrico De Angelis. Turin: Einaudi. Original title *Ästhetische Theorie* (Aesthetic theory), 1970.

– 1979. *Minima moralia: Meditazioni della vita offesa* (Minima moralia: Reflections from damaged life). Turin: Einaudi.

– 1997. "Functionalism Today." In *Rethinking Architecture*, edited by Neil Leach, translated by Newman and Smith, 6–19. New York: Routledge.

– 2008. "Architettura e utopia" (Architecture and utopia). In *Estetica e architettura* (Aesthetics and architecture), edited by Ettore Rocca, 158–70. Bologna: Il Mulino.

– 2011. *Parva aesthetica: Saggi 1956–1967* (Parva aesthetica: Essays 1956–1967), ed. R. Masiero. Milan: Mimesis.

Agamben, Giorgio. 1993. *The Coming Community*. Translated by Michael Hardi. Minneapolis: University of Minnesota Press.

– 2009. *What Is an Apparatus? And Other Essays*. Translated by David Kishik and Stefan Pedatella. Stanford, CA: Stanford University Press.

Alberti, Leon Battista. 1966. *De re aedificatoria* (On the art of building). Milan: Il Polifilo.

Alfieri, Luigi. 2003. "La paura e la città" (Fear and the city). In *Filosofia e emozioni* (Philosophy and the emotions), edited by Pasquale Venditti, 35–62. Florence: Le Monnier.

Amato, Pierandrea, and Federica Ferrara, eds. 2009. *Oscar Niemeyer: Architettura e filosofia* (Oscar Niemeyer: Architecture and philosophy). Rome: Aracne.

Ambasz, Emilio, ed. 2006. *The University Project: Solutions for Post-Technological Society*. New York: Museum of Modern Art.

Amendola, Giandomenico, ed. 2006. *La città vetrina: I luoghi del commercio e le nuove forme del consumo* (The display window city: Places for commerce and new forms of consumption). Naples: Liguori.

Appadurai, Arjun. 1996. *Modernity at Large*. Minneapolis: Minnesota University Press.

– 2013. *The Future as Cultural Fact: Essays on the Global Condition*. London: Verso.

Arendt, Hannah. 1958. *The Human Condition*. Chicago, IL: University of Chicago Press.

– 1990. *Teoria del giudizio politico* (A theory of political judgement). Genoa: Il Melangolo.

Aristotle. 1943. *Politics*. Translated by Benjamin Jowett. New York: Modern Library.

– 1959. *Art of Rhetoric*. Translated by John Henry Freese. Cambridge, MA: Harvard University Press.

Arsuaga, Juan Luis. 2002. *The Neanderthal's Necklace: In Search of a Lost World*. New York: Four Walls Eight Windows.

Assunto, Rosario. 1983. *La città di Anfione e la città di Prometeo: Idee e poetiche della città* (The city of Amphion and the city of Prometheus: Ideas and poetics of the city). Milan: Jaca Book.

Augé, Marc. 2007. *Tra i confini: Città, luoghi, interazioni* (Within borders: Cities, places, interactions). Milan: Bruno Mondadori.

– 2009. *Pour une anthropologie de la mobilité* (An anthropology of mobility). Paris: Payot & Rivages.

Bachelard, Gaston. 1964. *The Poetics of Space*. Translated by Maria Jolas. Boston: Beacon Press.

Bacon, Francis. 2000. *New Organon*. Cambridge, UK: Cambridge University Press.

Banham, Reyner. 2010. *Los Angeles: The Architecture of Four Ecologies*. Turin: Einaudi.

Barbagli, Marzio, and Maurizio Pisani. 2012. *Dentro e fuori le mura: Città e gruppi sociali dal 1400 a oggi* (Inside and outside the walls: Cities and social groups from 1400 to today). Bologna: Il Mulino.

Barnard, Alan. 2011. *Social Anthropology and Human Origins*. Cambridge: Cambridge University Press.

Barthes, Roland. 1967. "Semiologia e urbanistica" (Semiology and urbanism). *Op. cit: Selezione della critica d'arte contemporanea*, no. 10: 10–17.

– 1972. *Mythologies*. Translated by Annette Lavers. New York: Hill and Wang.

Baudelaire, Charles. 1964. *Petits poèmes en prose: Le spleen de Paris* (Short prose poems: Paris spleen). Edited by Henri Lemaître, 1964. Paris: Garnier Frères.

Baudrillard, Jean. 2000. *Les objets singuliers: Architecture et philosophie* (The singular objects of architecture). Paris: Calmann-Lévy.

– 2005. *The System of Objects*. Translated by James Benedict. London: Verso.

Bauman, Zygmunt. 2000. *Liquid Modernity*. Cambridge: Polity Press.

– 2005. *Fiducia e paura nella città* (Trust and fear in the city). Milan: Mondadori.

Bell, Daniel A., and Avner de-Shalit. 2011. *The Spirit of the Cities: Why the Identity of a City Matters in a Global Age*. Princeton, NJ: Princeton University Press.

Benevolo, Leonardo. 1963. *Le origini dell'urbanistca moderna* (The origins of modern urbanism). Rome-Bari: Laterza.

– 1993. *La città nella storia d'Europa* (The city in European history). Rome-Bari: Laterza.

– 2006. *Storia della città* (History of the city). 4 vols. Rome-Bari: Laterza.

– 2008. *L'architettura nel nuovo millennio* (Architecture in the new millennium). Rome-Bari: Laterza.

– 2011. *La fine della città* (The end of the city). Edited by Francesco Erbani. Rome-Bari: Laterza.

Benjamin, Walter. 1986. *Parigi, capitale del XIX secolo* (Paris, capital of the nineteenth century). Edited by Giorgio Agamben. Turin: Einaudi.

– 2000. *I "passages" di Parigi*. Turin: Einaudi. (*The Arcades Project*. Eng. trans. Howard Eiland. Cambridge, MA: Harvard University Press, 1999.)

– 2007. *Immagini di città* (Images of the city). Turin: Einaudi.

Berengo, Marino. 2010. *Città italiana e città europea* (Italian cities and European cities). Parma: Diabasis.

Berman, Marshall. 1982. *All That Is Solid Melts into Air*. New York: Simon and Schuster.

Berque, Augustin. 2010. *Milieu et identité humaine: Notes pour un dépassement de la modernité* (Milieu and human identity: Notes for surpassing modernity). Paris: Editions Donner Lieu.

Berque, Augustin, Alessia de Biase, and Philippe Bonnin, eds. 2012. *Donner lieu au monde: la poétique de l'habiter* (Giving place to the world: A poetics of dwelling). Proceedings of the Cerisy-la-Salle colloquium. Paris: Editions Donner Lieu.

Block, Marc Leopold Benjamin. 1953. *The Historian's Craft*. New York: Knopf.

Blumenberg, Hans. 1997. "Prospect for a Theory of Nonconceptuality." In *Shipwreck with Spectator: Metaphor of Paradigm for Existence*. Cambridge, MA: MIT Press.

Boas, George. 1944. "The City as a Work of Art." In *New Architecture and City Planning: A Symposium*, edited by Paul Zucker. New York: Philosophical Library.

Bodei, Remo. 2014. *La vita delle cose* (The life of things). Rome-Bari: Laterza.

Boeri, Stefano. 2011. *L'anticittà* (The anti-city). Rome-Bari: Laterza.

Borges, Jorge Luis. 2007. "Fervore di Buenos Aires" (Passion of Buenos Aires). In *La misura della mia speranza* (The size of my hope). Milan: Adelphi.

Bourdieu, Pierre. 1984. *Distinction: A Social Critique of the Judgement of Taste*. Translated by Richard Nice. Cambridge, MA: Harvard University Press.

Brandi, Cesare. 1996. *Scritti di architettura* (Essays on architecture). Edited by Giovanni Carbonara. Turin: Testo & Immagine.

– 2002. *Città del deserto* (Desert cities). Rome: Editori Riuniti.

Braudel, Fernand. 2013. *Venezia* (Venice). Bologna: Il Mulino.

Budett, Ricky, and Deyan Sudjic, eds. 2011. *Living in the Endless City*. London: Phaidon.

Butler, Judith. 2003. *Giving an Account of Oneself: A Critique of Ethical Violence*. Assen, Netherlands: Van Gorcum.

Cacciari, Massimo. 1973. *Saggio sulla grande città di Sombart, Endell, Sheffler e Simmel* (Essay on the great city for Sombart, Endell, Sheffer, and Simmel). Rome: Officina.

– 2004. *La città* (The city). Rimini: Pazzini.

Calthorpe, Peter. 2010. *Urbanism in the Age of Climate Change*. Washington, DC: Island Press.

Calvino, Italo. 1974. *Invisible Cities*. Translated by William Weaver. New York, NY: Harcourt Brace Jovanovich.

Canfora, Luciano. 2011. *Il mondo di Atene* (The Athenian world). Rome-Bari: Laterza.

Caracciolo, Alberto. 1982. *La città moderna e contemporanea* (The modern and contemporary city). Naples: Guida.

Carandini, Andrea, ed. 2013. *Atlante di Roma antica* (Atlas of ancient Rome). Milan: Electa.

Castells, Manuel. 2001. *The Internet Galaxy*. New York, London: Oxford University Press.

– 2004. *La città delle reti* (The network society). Venice: Marsilio.

Certeau, Michel de. 2002. *The Practice of Everyday Life*. Translated by Stephen Rendell. Berkeley, CA: University of California Press.

Cervellati, Pier Luigi. 1991. *La città bella* (The beautiful city). Bologna: Il Mulino.

Choay, Françoise. 1966. *L'Urbanisme, utopies et réalités* (Urbanism, utopias, and realities). Paris: Seuil.

– 1997. *The Rule and the Model: On the Theory of Architecture and Urbanism*. Cambridge, MA: MIT Press.

Ciorra, Pippo, and Sara Marini, eds. 2011. *Recycle: Strategie per l'architettura, la città e il pianeta* (Recycle: Strategies for architecture, the city, and the planet). Exhibit catalogue. Milan: Electa.

Ciucci, Giorgio. 2002. *Gli architetti e il fascismo: Architettura e città, 1922–1944* (Architects and fascism: Architecture and the city, 1922–1944). Turin: Einaudi.

Clément, Gilles. 2014. *Ho costruito una casa da giardiniere* (I have built as a gardener house). Macerata: Quodlibet.

Codeluppi, Vanni. 2014. *Metropoli e luoghi del consumo* (Metropoli and places of consumption). Milan: Mimesis.

Dal Co, Franco. 1985. *Abitare nel moderno* (Dwelling in modernity). Rome-Bari: Laterza.

D'Annunzio, Gabriele. 1924. "Dell'attenzione" (On attention). In *Faville del Maglio* (Sparks of the mallet). Vol. 1, *Il venturiero senza ventura* (Adventurer without adventure). Milan: Treves.

– 1976a. *Taccuni* (Notebooks). Edited by Enrica Bianchetti. Milan: Mondadori.

– 1976b. *Altri taccuini* (Other notebooks). Edited by Enrica Bianchetti. Milan: Mondadori.

Damisch, Hubert. 2001. *Skyline: The Narcissistic City*. Translated by John Goodman. Stanford, CA: Stanford University Press.

Danto, Arthur Coleman. 1981. *The Transfiguration of the Commonplace: A Philosophy of Art*. Cambridge, MA: Harvard University Press.

Davis, Mike. 1990. *City of Quartz: Excavating the Future in Los Angeles*. New York: Vintage Books.

– 1998. *Ecology of Fear: Los Angeles and the Imagination of Disaster*. New York: Vintage Books.

– 2006. *Planet of Slums*. London, New York: Verso.

De Benedetti, Mara, and Attilio Pracchi, eds. 1988. *Antologia dell'architettura moderna* (Anthology of modern architecture). Bologna: Zanichelli.

De Fusco, Renato. 2003. *Il codice dell'architettura: Antologia di trattatisti* (The code of architecture: An anthology of treatise writers). Naples: Liguori.

De Luca, Pina. 2014. *Visioni metropolitane* (Metropolitan vistas). Milan: Guerini.

De Seta, Cesare. 1999. *Città verso il 2000* (The city at the dawn of the year 2000). Milan: Mondadori.

– 2010. *La città europea* (The European city). Milan: Il Saggiatore.

De Seta, Cesare, ed. 1980. *Le città nella storia d'Italia* (Cities in the history of Italy). Rome-Bari: Laterza.

Deleuze, Gilles. 1992. *The Fold: Leibniz and the Baroque*. Translated by Tom Conley. Minneapolis: University of Minnesota Press.

Deleuze, Gilles, and Félix Guattari. 1987. *A Thousand Plateaus: Capitalism and Schizophrenia*. Translated by Brian Massumi. Minneapolis: Minnesota University Press.

Derrida, Jacques. 1982. *Margins of Philosophy*. Translated by Alan Bass. Chicago, IL: University of Chicago Press.

– 1987. *Psyché: Inventions de l'autre* (Psyche: Inventions of the other). Paris: Galilé.

– 1997a. "Point de Folie: Maintenant l'architecture." In *Rethinking Architecture*, edited by Neil Leach. New York: Routledge.

– 1997b. *Chora L Works*, edited by Jeffrey Kipnis and Thomas Leeser. New York: Monacelli Press.

– 2008. *Adesso l'architettura* (Now architecture). Edited by Francesco Vitale. Milan: Libri Scheiwiller.

Dewey, John. 1934. *Art as Experience*. New York: Minton.

Di Biagi, Paola. 1998. *La Carta di Atene: Manifesto e frammento dell'urbanistica moderna* (The Athens Charter: A manifesto and fragment of modern urbanism). Rome: Officina.

Di Branco, Marco. 2006. *La città dei filosofi: Storia di Atene da Marco Aurelio a Giustiniano* (The city of philosophers: History of Athens from Marcus Aurelius to Justinian). Florence: Olschki.

Di Palma, Vittorio, Diana Periton, and Marina Lathouri. 2009. *Intimate Metropolis*. London: Routledge.

Diderot, Denis. 1988. *L'estetica dell'Encyclopédie* (Aesthetics of the encyclopèdie). Edited by Massimo Modica. Rome: Editori Riuniti.

Doglio, Carlo. 1985. *La città giardino: Crisi dell'utopia, città e urbanistica di fronte alla rivoluzione industriale.* (The garden city: Crisis of utopia, the city, and urbanism in the Industrial Revolution). Rome: Cangemi.

Dorfles, Gillo. 1968. *Il Kitsch* (Kitsch). Milan: Mazzotta.

– 1972. *L'architettura moderna* (Modern architecture). Milan: Garzanti.

– 2008. *Horror pleni* (Fear of full spaces). Rome: Castelvecchi.

Dufrenne, Mikel. 1981. "Arte e natura" (Art and nature). In *Trattato di estetica* (Treatise on architecture), by Mikel Dufrenne and Dino Formaggio. 2 vols. Milan: Mondadori.

– 1989. "Le Cap Ferrat" (Cape Ferrat). In *Revue d'Esthétique*, no. 16.

Duque, Félix. 2008. *Habitar la tierra* (Inhabiting the earth). Madrid: Abada.

Eco, Umberto. 1994. *Apocalypse Postponed*. Edited by Robert Lumley. Bloomington, IN: Indiana University Press.

Eggers, Dave. 2013. *The Circle: A Novel*. New York: Knopf.

Enciclopedia Einaudi (Encyclopedia Einaudi). 1990. Vol. 3: Città-Cosmologie. Turin: Einaudi. 3–84.

Falqui, Laura. 2014. *Forme e materiali della città fantastica* (Forms and materials of the imagined city). Milan: Franco Angeli.

Ferlenga, Alberto, ed. 2013. *L'Architettura del mondo: Infrastrutture, mobilità, nuovi paesaggi* (World architecture: Infrastructures, mobility, new landscapes). Exhibit catalogue, Triennale di Milano. Milan: Editrice Compositori.

Filoni, Marco. 2014. *Lo spazio inquieto: La città e la paura* (The space of disquiet: The city and fear). Palermo: Edizioni Passaggio.

Finocchiaro, Emma. 1999. *Città in trasformazione: Le logiche di sviluppo della metropoli contemporanea* (Cities in transition: The logic of growth in the contemporary metropolis). Milan: Franco Angeli.

Florida, Richard. 2005. *Cities and the Creative Class*. London: Routledge.

Focillon, Henri. 1987. *Vita delle forme*. Turin: Einaudi. (*The Life of Forms in Art*. Eng. trans. George Kubler. New York: Zone Books, 1989.)

Foucault, Michel. 1997. "Of Other Spaces: Utopias and Heterotopias." In *Rethinking Architecture: A Reader in Cultural Theory*, edited by Neil Leach, 330–36. New York: Routledge.

– 2001. *Il discorso, la storia, la verità: Interventi 1969–1984* (Discourse, history, truth: Essays 1969–1984). Edited by Maurizio Bettini. Turin: Einaudi.

Frisby, David. 1988. *Fragments of Modernity: Theories of Modernity in Simmel, Kracauer, Benjamin*. Cambridge, MA: MIT Press.

Frisby, David, and Mike Featherstone, eds. 1997. *Georg Simmel on Culture: Selected Writings*. London: Sage.

Frugoni, Chiara. 1983. *Una lontana città: Sentimenti e immagini nel medioevo* (A far away city: Feelings and images in the Middle Ages). Turin: Einaudi.

Fumagalli, Vita. 1999. *La pietra viva: Città e natura nel Medioevo* (Natural stone: The city and nature in the Middle Ages). Bologna: Il Mulino.

Gadamer, Hans Georg. 1986. *Attualità del bello* (The relevance of the beautiful). Genoa: Marietti.

– 1990. *Verità e metodo* (Truth and method). Milan: Bompiani.

Gehl, Jan. 2010. *Cities for People*. Washington, DC: Island Press.

Gehlen, Arnold. 1980. *Man in the Age of Technology*. Translated by Patricia Lipscomb. New York: Columbia University Press.

Giedion, Siegfried. 1948. *Mechanization Takes Command: A Contribution to Anonymous History*. New York: Oxford University Press.

– 1964. *The Eternal Present: A Contribution on Constancy and Change*. Oxford, UK: Oxford University Press.

– 2008. *Breviario di architettura* (Handbook of architecture). Edited by Carlo Olmo: Turin: Bollati Borighieri.

Glaeser, Edward. 2011. *Triumph of the City*. New York: Penguin Press.

Goffmann, Erving. 1959. *The Presentation of Self in Everyday Life*. New York: Doubleday.

Greco, Emanuele, and Mario Torelli. 1983. *Storia dell'urbanistica: Il mondo greco* (History of urbanism: The Greek world). Rome-Bari: Laterza.

Gregotti, Vittorio. 2008. *Contro la fine dell'architettura* (Against the end of architecture). Turin: Einaudi.

– 2011. *Architettura e postmetropoli* (Architecture and postmetropolis). Turin: Einaudi.

Gros, Pietro, and Mario Torelli. 1988. *Storia dell'urbanistica: Il mondo romano* (History of urban planning: The Roman world). Rome-Bari: Laterza.

Guidoni, Enrico. 1970. *La città europea: Formazione e significato dal IV all'XI secolo* (The European city: Formation and meaning from the 4th to the 11th century). Milan: Electa.

Hall, Peter. 1998. *Cities in Civilization*. New York: Pantheon Books.

Halliwell, Stephen. 2002. *The Aesthetics of Mimesis: Ancient Texts and Modern Problems*. Princeton, NJ: Princeton University Press.

Hannerz, Ulf. 1980. *Exploring the City: Inquiries Toward an Anthropology of Urban Life*. New York: Columbia University Press.

Harries, Karsten. 1997. *The Ethical Function of Architecture*. Cambridge, MA: MIT Press.

Harvey, David. 1989. *The Urban Experience*. Oxford, UK: Basil Blackwell.

– 2010. *The Enigma of Capital and the Crises of Capitalism*. New York, London: Oxford University Press.

– 2012. *Il capitalismo contro il diritto alla città: Neoliberalismo, urbanizzazione, resistenze* (Capitalism against the right to the city: Neoliberalism, urbanization, resistance). Milan: Ombre Corte.

– 2014. *Seventeen Contradictions and the End of Capitalism*. New York: Oxford University Press.

Hegel, Georg Wilhelm Friedrich. 1967. *Estetica* (Aesthetics). Edited by Nicolao Merker. Turin: Einaudi.

Heidegger, Martin. 1988. *L'arte e lo spazio* (Art and space). Genoa: Il Melangolo.

– 1993. "Building, Dwelling, Thinking." In *Basic Writings*, edited by David Farrel Krell, 343–64. San Francisco: HarperSanFrancisco.

– 2001. "Hölderlin e l'essenza della poesia" (Hölderlin and the essence of poetry). In *La poesia di Hölderlin* (The poetry of Hölderlin). Milan: Adelphi.

Herodotus. 1987–1997. *Historiae*. Edited by Halim B. Rosen. Leipzig: Teubner.

Herzog, Jacques, and Pierre de Meuron. 2014. *Natural History*. Zurich: Lars Muller.

Illich, Ivan. 1973. *Tools for Conviviality*. New York: Harper and Rowe.

Il patrimonio e l'abitare (Patrimony and dwelling). 2010. Curated by Carmen Andriani. Rome: Donzelli.

Indovina, Francesco, ed. 2009. *Dalla città diffusa all'arcipelago americano* (From the diffused city to the American archipelago). Milan: Franco Angeli.

Ingarden, Roman. 1962. *Untersuchungen zur Ontologie der Kunst* (Ontology of the work of art). Tübingen: Max Niemeyer.

Ingold, Tim. 2001. *Ecologia della cultura* (The ecology of culture). Rome: Meltemi.

– 2013. *Making Anthropology, Archeology, Art, and Architecture*. London: Routledge.

Innerarity, Daniel. 2006. *El nuevo espacio público* (The new public space). Madrid: Espasa.

Ippolito, Achille Maria, ed. 2013. *Il paesaggio urbano contemporaneo* (The contemporary urban landscape). Milan: Franco Angeli.

Jabès, Edmondo. 1991. *Il libro dell'ospitalità* (The book of hospitality). Milan: Raffaello Cortina.

Jacobs, Jane. 1961. *The Death and Life of Great American Cities*. New York: Random House.

Jencks, Charles. 2011. *The Story of Post-Modernism: Five Decades of the Ironic, Iconic and Critical in Architecture*. Chichester, UK: John Wiley and Sons.

Jenkins, Paul, and Leslie Forsyth, eds. 2009. *Architecture, Participation, and Society*. London: Routledge.

Johnson, Philip. 1985. *Verso il postmoderno: Genesi di una deregulation creativa* (On the postmodern: Genesis of a creative deregulation). Genoa: Costa and Nolan.

Jullien, François. 2011. *The Silent Transformations*. Chicago, IL: University of Chicago Press.

Kant, Immanuel. 1987. *Critique of Judgment*. Translated by Werner S. Pluhar. Indiannapolis-Cambridge: Hackett.

Koolhaas, Rem. 1995. "Singapore Songlines: Portrait of a Potemkin Metropolis … Or Thirty Years of Tabula Rasa." In *S,M,L,XL*. New York: Monacelli Press.

– 2006a. *Junkspace: Per un ripensamento radicale dello spazio urbano* (Junkspace: For a radical rethinking of urban space). Edited by Gabriele Mastrigli. Macerata: Quodlibet.

– 2006b. *Bigness*. Macerata: Quodlibet.

– 2014. *Fundamentals: Fourteenth International on Architecture Exhibition*. Venice: Marsilio.

Kracauer, Siegfried. 1996. *The Mass Ornament: Weimar Essays*. Cambridge, MA: Harvard University Press.

Kruft, Hanno-Walter. 1994. *A History of Architectural Theory from Vitruvius to the Present*. Translated by Ronald Taylor, Elsie Callander, and Anthony Wood. New York: Princeton Architectural Press.

La Cecla, Franco. 2008. *Contro l'architettura* (Against architecture). Turin: Bollati Boringhieri.

– 2011. *Mente locale: Per un'antropologia dell'abitare* (Local mind: An anthropology of dwelling). Milan: Eleuthera.

– 2015. *Contro l'urbanistica* (Against urbanism). Turin: Einaudi.

Lambertini, Anna, ed. 2014. *The Role of Open Spaces*. Bologna: Editrice Compositori.

Le Corbusier (Charles-Édouard Jeanneret). 1994. *Urbanisme* (Urbanism). Paris: Flammarion.

Lees, Loretta, Tom Slater, and Elvin K. Wyly. 2008. *Gentrification*. London: Routledge.

Lefebvre, Henri. 1976. *Spazio e politica: il diritto alla città* (Space and politics: The right to the city). Milan: Moizzi.

Le Goff, Jacques. 1982. "L'immaginario urbano nell'Italia medievale" (The urban imaginary in medieval Italy). In *Storia d'Italia* (History of Italy). Vol. 5: *Il paesaggio* (The landscape). Turin: Einaudi.

Leone, Massimo, ed. 2008. *Città come testo: Scritture e riscritture urbane* (The city as text: Urban writings and re-writings). Rome: Aracne.

Lévinas, Emmanuel. 1979. *Totality and Infinity: An Essay on Exteriority*. Translated by Alphonso Lingis. The Hague-Boston-London: Martinus Nijhoff Publisher.

Lizzani, Francesco, and Laura Ricca. 2012. *Dalla città celeste al labirinto metropolitano* (From the heavenly city to the metropolitan labyrinth). Imola: La Mandragora.

Loraux, Nicole. 2002. *The Divided City: On Memory and Forgetting in Ancient Athens*. Translated by Corinne Ondine Pache. New York: Zone Books.

Löwith, Karl. 1949. *Meaning in History: The Theological Implications of the Philosophy of History*. Chicago, IL: University of Chicago Press.

Lucan, Marcus Antonius. 2015. *Civil War*. Translated by Brian Walters. Cambridge, MA: Hackett.

Luhmann, Niklas. 1998. *Observations on Modernity*. Translated by William Whobery. Stanford, CA: Stanford University Press.

Lynch, Kevin. 1960. *The Image of the City*. Cambridge, MA: MIT Press.

Maffesoli, Michel. 2000. *Del nomadismo: Per una sociologia dell'errare* (On nomadism: For a sociology of wandering). Milan: Franco Angeli.

– 2007. *Le Réenchantement du monde* (The re-enchantment of the world). Paris: Table Ronde.

– 2010. *Apocalisse: Rivelazioni sulla società postmoderna* (The apocalypse: Revelations on postmodern society). Naples: Ipermedium.

Maffi, Mario. 2014. *Città di memoria* (Cities of memory). Milan: Il Saggiatore.

Marche, Marzia. 2008. *Metropoli asiatiche in trasformazione: Seul, Shangai, Hanoi.* (Asian metropoli in transformation: Seoul, Shanghai, Hanoi). Rome: Carocci.

Marrone, Gianfranco. 2013. *Figure di città: Spazi urbani e discorsi sociali* (Images of the city: Urban spaces and social discourses). Milan: Mimesis.

Marrone, Gianfranco, and Isabella Pezzini, eds. 2008. *Senso e metropoli* (Sense and metropoli). Rome: Meltemi.

Masiero, Roberto. 1999. *Estetica dell'architettura* (Aesthetics of architecture). Bologna: Il Mulino.

Mastropietro, Eleonora. 2013. *Città e aree metropolitane europee tra trasformazioni urbane e progetti per la sostenibilità* (European cities and metropolitan areas from urban transformations to sustainability projects). Milan: Mimesis.

Mattogno, Claudia, ed. 2002. *Idee di spazio: Lo spazio delle idee – Metropoli contemporanee e spazi pubblici* (Ideas of space: The space of ideas – Contemporary metropoli and public spaces). Milan: Franco Angeli.

McLuhan, Marshall. 1964. *Understanding Media: The Extensions of Man*. New York: New American Library.

Meier, Richard L. 1962. *Communication Theory of Urban Growth*. Cambridge, MA: MIT Press.

Meier, Christian, and Paul Veyne. 1989. *L'identità del cittadino e la democrazia in Grecia* (The identity of the citizen and democracy in Greece). Bologna: Il Mulino.

Merleau-Ponty, Maurice. 1965. *Phenomenology of Perception*. Translated by Colin Smith. London: Routledge.

Mills, Charles Wright. 1961. *Images of Man: The Classic Tradition in Sociological Thinking*. New York: G. Brasiller.

Modica, Massimo, ed. 1988. *L'Estetica dell'Encyclopédie* (The aesthetics of the encyclopedia). Rome: Riuniti Editori.

Moretti, Franco. 1987. *Segni e stili del moderno* (Signs and styles of modernity). Turin: Einaudi.

Morris, Anthony Edwin James. 1979. *History of Urban Form: Before the Industrial Revolution*. New York: Wiley.

Morris, William. 1908. *News from Nowhere.* London: Longmans.

Moussavi, Farshid, and Michael Kubo, eds. 2006. *The Function of Ornament*. Barcelona and Cambridge: Actar and Harvard Graduate School of Design.

– 2009. *The Function of Form*. Barcelona and Cambridge: Actar and Harvard Graduate School of Design.

Mumford, Lewis. 1922. *The Story of Utopias*. New York: Boni and Liveright.

– 1938. *The Culture of Cities*. New York: Harcourt Brace and Company.

– 1961. *The City in History*. San Diego, CA: Harcourt.

– 1966. *Arte e tecnica* (Art and technics). Milan: Etas Kompas.

Nancy, Jean Luc. 2011. *La ville au loin* (The far away city). Paris: Phocide.

Nietzsche, Friedrich Wilhelm. 1970. *Crepuscolo degli idoli* (Twilight of the idols). In *Opere* (Complete works). Vol. 6, tome 3. Edited by Giorgio Colli and Maurizio Montinari. Milan: Adelphi.

– 1986. *Human, All Too Human*. Translated by Reginald John. Hollingdale. Cambridge, MA: Cambridge University Press.

– 2010. *Thus Spake Zarathustra*. Translated by Thomas Common, edited by Bill Chapko. Feedbooks.

Norberg-Schulz, Christian. 1980. *Genius Loci: Towards a Phenomenology of Architecture*. New York: Rizzoli.

Nuvolati, Giampaolo. 2013. *L'interpretazione dei luoghi: Flânerie come esperienza di vita* (The interpretation of places: Flânerie as life experience). Florence: Florence University Press.

Olmo, Carlo, ed. 2000. *Dizionario dell'architettura del XX secolo* (Dictionary of twentieth-century architecture). Turin: Allemandi.

Ottinger, Didier, and Quentin Bajc. 2010. *Dreamlands: Des parcs d'attraction aux cités du future* (Dreamlands: Amusement parks in the cities of the future). Paris: Centre Pompidou.

Paci, Enzo. 2007. "L'architettura e il mondo della vita" (Architecture and life). In *Aut Aut, no. 333*. Milan: Il Saggiatore.

Palladio, Andrea. 1965. *The Four Books of Architecture*. New York: Dover.

Panofsky, Erwin. 1957. *Gothic Architecture and Scholasticism*. New York: Meridian Books.

– 1968. *Idea: A Concept of Art Theory*. Translated by Joseph J.S. Peak. New York: Harper and Rowe.

Panza, Pierluigi. 1996. *Estetica dell'architettura* (Aesthetics of architecture). Milan: Guerini.

Papi, Fulvio. 2000. *Filosofia e architettura: Kant, Hegel, Valéry, Heidegger, Derrida* (Philosophy and architecture: Kant, Hegel, Valéry, Heidegger, Derrida). Como-Pavia: Ibis.

Park, Robert Ezra, Ernest W. Burgess, and Roderick D. McKenzie. 1969. *The City*. Chicago, IL: Chicago University Press.

Pausanias. 1918–1935. *Description of Greece*. 4 vols. Cambridge, MA: Harvard University Press.

Payor, Daniel. 1982. *Le Philosophe et l'architecte* (The philosopher and the architect). Paris: Aubier.

Perec, Georges. 1997. *Species of Spaces and Other Pieces*. Translated by John Sturrock. New York: Penguin.

Petrillo, Agostino. 2000. *La città perduta: L'eclissi della dimensione umana nel mondo contemporaneo* (The lost city: Eclipse of the human dimension in the contemporary world). Bari: Dedalo.

Pevsner, Nikolas. 1959. *L'architettura moderna e il design: Da William Morris alla Bauhaus* (Modern architecture and design: From William Morris to the Bauhaus). Turin: Einaudi.

Phaidon. 2013. *Atlante mondiale dell'architectura del XX secolo* (Atlas of twentieth-century world architecture). Milan: Electa/Phaidon.

Piano, Renzo. 2010. *La responsabilità dell'architetto: Conversazione con Renzo Cassigoli* (The responsibility of the architect: A conversation with Renzo Cassigoli). Florence: Passigli.

Pignatti, Lorenza. 2013. "Beirut la città postbellica e la sua topografia porosa" (Beirut the post-war city and its porous topography). *Parol*, no. 23: 196–208.

Pindar. 1961. *Odes with Principal Fragments*. Translated by Sir John Sandys. Cambridge, MA: Harvard University Press.

Pirenne, Henri. 1956. *Medieval Cities: Their Origins and the Revival of Trade*. Translated by Frank D. Halsey. Garden City, NY: Doubleday.

Plato. 1960. *Laws*. Translated by Alfred Edward Taylor. London: Dent.

– 1989. *Symposium*. Translated by Christopher Gill. London, New York: Penguin.

Portoghesi, Paolo. 1980. *Dopo l'architettura moderna* (After modern architecture). Rome-Bari: Laterza.

– 2005. *Geoarchitettura: Verso un'architettura della responsabilità* (Geoarchitecture: Towards an architecture of responsibility). Milan: Skira.

Prakash, Gyan. 2012. *La città color zafferano: Bombay tra metropoli e mito* (The saffron-coloured city: Bombay between metropolis and myth). Milan: Bruno Mondadori.

Pugin, Augustus Welby Northmore. 2011. *Contrasts, and the True Principles of Pointed or Christian Architecture*. Reading: Spire Books.

Ratti, Carlo. 2014. *Architettura Open Source: Verso una progettazione aperta* (Open source architecture: On open planning). Turin: Einaudi.

Ricœur, Paul. 1977. *The Rule of Metaphor*. Translated by Robert Czerny. Toronto: University of Toronto Press.

– 2008. "Architettura e narratività" (Architecture and narrativity). In *Estetica e architettura* (Aesthetics and architecture), edited by Ettore Rocca, 235–49. Bologna: Il Mulino.

Riesman, David. 1956. *The Lonely Crowd: A Study of the Changing American Character*. New Haven, CT: Yale University Press.

Ripellino, Angelo Maria. 1961. Preface to *Pietroburgo* (Petersburg), by Andrei Belyi. Turin: Einaudi.

Riva, Franco, ed. 2008. *Leggere la città: Quattro testi di Paul Ricœur* (Reading the city: Four Paul Ricœur texts). Rome: Città aperta.

Rocca, Ettore, ed. 2008. *Estetica e architettura* (Aesthetics and architecture). Bologna: Il Mulino.

Romano, Marco. 1993. *L'estetica della città europea* (Aesthetics of the European city). Turin: Einaudi.

– 2008. *La città come opera d'arte* (The city as work of art). Turin: Einaudi.

Rosa, Harmut. 2005. *Beschleunigung: Die Veränderung der Zeitstrukturen in der Moderne* (Acceleration: Changes in the structure of time in modernity). Frankfurt: Suhrkamp.

Rossi, Aldo. 2012. *L'architettura della città* (Urban architecture). Macerata: Quodlibet.

Rossi, Pietro, ed. 1987. *Modelli di città* (Model cities). Turin: Einaudi.

Rudofsky, Bernard. 1979. *Le meraviglie dell'architettura spontanea* (The wonders of spontaneous architecture). Rome-Bari: Laterza.

Ruskin, John. 1908. *The Stones of Venice*. New York: E.P. Dutton.

Rykwert, Joseph. 1976. *The Idea of a Town: The Anthropology of Urban Form in Rome, Italy, and the Ancient World*. Princeton, NJ: Princeton University Press.

– 2000. *The Seduction of Place: The History and Future of Cities*. New York: Pantheon.

Sadler, Simon. 1999. *The Situationist City*. Cambridge, MA: MIT Press.

Sansot, Pierre. 1984. *Poétique de la ville* (Poetics of the city). Paris: Klincksieck.

Scagliola, Stefano. 2013. "*Polis* e mito: Il *nomos* di Atene," (*Polis* and myth: The *nomos* of Athens). *Parol*, no. 23: 42–51.

Scamozzi, Vincenzo. 1982. *L'idea dell'architettura universale* (The idea of universal architecture). Sala Bolognese: Forni.

Schelling, Friedrich Wilhelm Joseph. 1986. *Filosofia dell'arte* (The philosophy of art) Edited by A. Klein. Naples: Prismi.

Scherrer, Franck, and Martin Vanier, eds. 2013. *Villes, térritoires, réversibilités* (Towns, territories, reversibilities). Proceedings of the colloques de Cerisy, 4–10 September, 2010. Paris: Hermann.

Schmitt, Carl. 2003. *The Nomos of the Earth*. Translated by G.I. Ulmen. New York: Telos Press.

Schopenhauer, Arthur. 1958. *The World as Will and Representation*. Translated by E.F.J. Payne. Indian Hills, CO: Falcon's Wing Press.

Sclavi, Marianella, ed. 2002. *Avventure urbane: Progettare la città con gli abitanti* (Urban adventures: Planning the city with inhabitants). Milan: Eleuthera.

Scruton, Roger. 1979. *The Aesthetics of Architecture*. Princeton, NJ: Princeton University Press.

– 2010. *Beauty*. Oxford: Oxford University Press.

Secchi, Bernardo. 2005. *La città del XX secolo* (The city in the twentieth century). Rome-Bari: Laterza.

– 2007. *Prima lezione di urbanistica* (First lesson in urbanism). Rome-Bari: Laterza.

– 2013. *La città dei ricchi e la città dei poveri* (The city of the rich and the city of the poor). Rome-Bari: Laterza.

Sedlmayr, Hans. 1958. *Art in Crisis: The Lost Centre*. Chicago, IL: Regner.

Sennett, Richard. 1970. *The Uses of Disorder: Personal Identity and City Life*. New York: Knopf.

Serres, Michel. 1991. *Rome: The Book of Foundations*. Translated by Felicia McCarren. Stanford, CA: Stanford University Press.

Sgarbi, Claudio, ed. 2004. *Vitruvio ferrarese: De architectura* (Vitruvius and Ferrara: On architecture). Preface by Joseph Rykwert. Modena: Panini.

Shu, Wang. 2013. *Construire un monde différent conforme aux principes de la nature* (Building a different world in accordance with the principles of nature). Paris: Editions des Cendres.

Sica, Paolo. 1980. *Storia dell'urbanistica* (History of urbanism). Rome-Bari: Laterza.

Silber, John. 2007. *Architecture of the Absurd: How "Genius" Disfigured a Practical Art*. New York: Quantum Lane Press.

Simmel, Georg. 1970. "Ponte e porta" (Bridge and door). In *Saggi di estetica* (Essays on aesthetics), edited by Massimo Cacciari. Padua: Liviana.

– 1987. "Il dominio della tecnica" (The predominance of technology). In *Tecnica e cultura: Il dibattito tedesco tra Bismark e Weimar* (Technology and culture: The German debate between Bismark and Weimar), edited by Tomás Maldonado, 37–46. Milan: Feltrinelli.

– 1995. *La metropoli e la vita dello spirito* (The metropolis and mental life). Rome: Armando.

Soleri, Paolo. 1969. *Arcology: The City in the Image of Man*. Cambridge, MA: MIT Press.

Sophocles. 1948. *Oedipus at Colonus*. Translated by Gilbert Murray. London: Allen and Unwin.

Spengler, Oswald. 1981. *Il tramonto dell'Occidente: Lineamenti di una morfologia della Storia universale*. Edited by Furio Jesi. Milan: Longanesi. (*The Decline of the West*. Eng. trans. Charles Francis Atkinson. New York: Knopf, 1966.)

Spinoza, Benedict de. 1963. *Ethics*. Edited by James Gutmann. New York: Hafner.

Spivak, Gayatri Chakravorty. 1999. *A Critique of Postcolonial Reason*. Cambridge, MA: Harvard University Press.

Steenbergen, Clement, and Wouter Reh. 2011. *Metropolitan Landscape Architecture: Urban Parks and Landscapes*. Springfield: Thoth.

Strauss, Leo. 2010. *La città e l'uomo* (The city and man) Milan: Marietti.

Sussen, Saskia. 1997. *Città globali: New York, London, Tokyo* (The global city: New York, London, Tokyo). Turin: UTET.

Tafuri, Manfredo. 1987. *The Sphere and the Labyrinth: Avant-gardes and Architecture from Piranesi to the 1970s*. Translated by Pellegrino d'Acierno and Robert Connoly. Cambridge, MA: MIT Press.

Tagliaventi, Gabriele. 1994. *Garden Cities: A Century of Ideas, Projects, Experiences*. Rome: Gangemi.

Tattersall, Ian. 2013. *I signori del pianeta: La ricerca delle origini dell'uomo* (Masters of the planet: The search for our human origins). Turin: Codice.

Taylor, Peter. 2003. *World Cities Network*. London: Routledge.

Thucydides. 1954. *History of the Peloponnesian War*. Translated by Sir Richard Livingstone. London: Oxford University Press.

Tosco, Carlo. 2011. *Petrarca: Paesaggi, città, architetture* (Petrarch: Landscapes, cities, architecture). Rome: Quodlibet.

Trione, Vincenzo. 2014. *Effetto città* (City effect). Milan: Bompiani.

Valéry, Paul. 1990. *Eupalinos ou l'Architecte* (Eupalinos or the architect). In *Tre dialoghi* (Three dialogues). Ital. trans. Vittorio Sereni. Turin: Einaudi.

Vasari, Giorgio. 1970. *La città ideale* (The ideal city). Edited by Virginia Stefanelli. Rome: Officina.

Vegetti, Matteo, ed. 2009. *Filosofie della metropoli* (Philosophies of the metropolis). Rome: Carocci.

Venturi, Robert, Denise Scott Brown, and Steven Izenour. 1977. *Learning from Las Vegas*. Cambridge, MA: MIT Press.

Véron, Jacques. 2008. *L'urbanizzazione del mondo* (The urbanization of the world). Bologna: Il Mulino.

Vicari Haddock, Serena, ed. 2011. *Questioni urbane* (Urban issues). Bologna: Il Mulino.

Virilio, Paul. 2004. *Città panico: L'altrove comincia qui* (City of panic: Elsewhere begins here). Milan: Raffaello Cortina.

– 2011. *L'arte dell'accecamento* (The art of blinding). Milan: Raffaello Cortina.

Weber, Max. 1968. *Economy and Society: An Outline of Interpretive Sociology*. Translated by Ephraim Fishoff. New York: Bedminister Press.

– 1979. *La città* (The city). Milan: Bompiani.

– 1995. *Considerazioni intermedie: Il destino dell'occidente* (Intermediate reflections: The destiny of the west). Edited by Alessandro Ferrara. Rome: Armando.

Wheatley, Paul. 1969. *City as Symbol: An Inaugural Lecture Delivered at University College, London, 20 November 1967*. London: H.K. Lewis.

Wikan, Unni. 2014. *Resonance: Beyond the Words*. Chicago, IL: University of Chicago Press.

Wines, James. 2000. *Green Architecture*. Köln: Taschen.

Winters, Edward. 2007. *Aesthetics and Architecture*. London: Continuum.

Wirth, Louis. 1938. *Urbanism as a Way of Life*. Indianapolis: Bobbs-Merrill.

Wittgenstein, Ludwig. 1980. *Pensieri diversi* (Thoughts). Milan: Adelphi.

Wittkower, Rudolf. 1949. *Architectural Principles in the Age of Humanism*. London: Warburg Institute, University of London.

– 1968. *Art and Architecture in Italy, 1600–1750*. Baltimore: Penguin.

Wölfflin, Heinrich. 1999. *Prolegomena zu einer Psychologie der Architektur* (Prologomena to a psychology of architecture). Gebr. Mann.

Wright, Frank Lloyd. 1963. *Testamento* (A testament). Turin: Einaudi.

Xenophon. 1994. *Memorabilia*. Translated by Amy L. Bonnette. Ithaca, NY: Cornell University Press.

Zanker, Paul. 2013. *La città romana* (The Roman city). Rome-Bari: Laterza.

Zevi, Bruno. 1950. *Storia dell'architettura moderna* (History of modern architecture). Turin: Einaudi.

Zukin, Sharon. 1995. *The Culture of the Cities*. Cambridge, MA: Blackwell.

Zumthor, Paul. 1993. *La mesure du monde: Représentation de l'espace au Moyen Age* (World measures: Representation of space in the Middle Ages). Paris: Seuil.

Index